OFFICE OF THE CHAIRMAN

May 21, 1991

Honorable Evan J. Kemp, Jr.
Chairman
Equal Employment Opportunity Commission
Washington, D.C.

Dear Mr. Kemp:

The Committee on Mandatory Retirement in Higher Education was charged with examining the potential effects on colleges and universities and faculty members of ending the current exemption for tenured faculty in the Age Discrimination in Employment Act. In estimating the potential effects of no longer allowing a m^~ ⌐ v retirement age of 70 for faculty, the committee has ⌐ 'ty demographic trends, evidence on age and pe^f retirement policies, both at institution^ ory retirement already and those that

The committee concludes th _ence does not justify continuing the exem ⌐om the overall federal policy of prohibiting i _.ent on the basis of age. The committee notes, however, _.ange will not have consistent effects across the college anu university community. The committee concludes that this change is unlikely to affect the vast majority of colleges and universities because most faculty members now retire well before age 70. At a few research universities, however, a high proportion of faculty now work until age 70, and they may well choose to work past that age if mandatory retirement is eliminated.

In order to play their key role in maintaining the cutting edge of American science, research universities need constant reinvigoration of their faculties, particularly through the addition of scholars in emerging fields. Faculty turnover has traditionally given universities the flexiblity to hire in developing fields. With the diminished turnover likely from the elimination of mandatory retirement for older faculty members, it will be more costly for these research universities to hire new faculty.

THE NATIONAL RESEARCH COUNCIL IS THE PRINCIPAL OPERATING AGENCY OF THE NATIONAL ACADEMY OF SCIENCES AND
THE NATIONAL ACADEMY OF ENGINEERING TO SERVE GOVERNMENT AND OTHER ORGANIZATIONS

The committee has examined the issue of faculty turnover and concludes that a number of actions can be taken by affected universities to encourage rather than mandate selected faculty retirements. Though not cost free, the proposed changes are likely to enhance faculty turnover. Foremost among them is the use of retirement incentive programs, common in industry and now becoming more widely implemented in higher education. The committee calls on Congress and the relevant agencies to "permit colleges and universities to offer faculty voluntary retirement incentive programs that: are not classified as an employee benefit, include an upper age limit for participants, and limit participation on the basis of institutional needs." The committee also recommends policies that would allow universities to change their pension, health, and other benefit programs in response to changing faculty retirement behavior and needs.

The costs of such programs will not be easy for research universities to shoulder, especially in the context of a number of other factors that are exerting intense financial pressure on them. Increased need for financial aid has largely been met by institutional funds; research instrumentation and facilities need upgrading and replacement; new tax laws have limited fund raising; tax-exempt borrowing has been curtailed; expensive benefit program changes have resulted from recent tax and accounting regulations; and tuition increases are encountering increased resistance. In this context, the nation's research universities may have difficulty finding room in their budgets for even small cost increases resulting from the elimination of mandatory retirement.

Thus, we draw particular attention to the committee's recommendations calling on Congress and regulatory agencies to assist research universities in minimizing the potential adverse effects of eliminating mandatory retirement for tenured faculty. These universities support work at the very heart of the American system of basic research. The committee has recommended policies that are sensitive to the importance of that system, as well as to national policy on age discrimination.

Sincerely yours,

Robert McC. Adams, Chairman
Commission on Behavioral and Social
   Sciences and Education
National Research Council

Frank Press
Chairman
National Research Council

# ENDING MANDATORY RETIREMENT FOR TENURED FACULTY

## The Consequences for Higher Education

P. Brett Hammond and Harriet P. Morgan, *Editors*

Committee on Mandatory Retirement
in Higher Education

Ralph E. Gomory, *Chair*

Commission on Behavioral and Social Sciences
and Education

National Research Council

NATIONAL ACADEMY PRESS
Washington, D.C. 1991

The project that is the subject of this book was supported by the U.S. Equal Employment Opportunity Commission.

Library of Congress Catalog Card No. 91-61424
International Standard Book Number 0-309-04498-7

Additional copies of this report are available from:

National Academy Press
2101 Constitution Avenue, N.W.
Washington, D.C. 20418

S355

Printed in the United States of America

# COMMITTEE ON MANDATORY RETIREMENT
# IN HIGHER EDUCATION

# Contents

# TABLES AND FIGURES

## Tables

## Figures

# Preface

As part of the 1986 amendments to the Age Discrimination in Employment Act (ADEA) prohibiting mandatory retirement ages for most workers,
Congress permitted colleges and universities to continue requiring tenured
faculty members to retire at age 70 until 1994. It did so in response to two
concerns from parts of the higher education community:  (1) postponed
faculty retirements would prevent colleges and universities from hiring new
faculty who are traditionally a source of new ideas, and (2) an aging professoriate would grow increasingly ineffective but unremovable because of
tenure.  Either of these possibilities could adversely affect the quality of
research and teaching in the nation's colleges and universities.  In particular, those who recognize the importance of strengthening the nation's basic
research system were concerned about the effects on the research universities of having more older faculty members.

In granting higher education an extension of mandatory retirement, Congress
directed the U.S. Equal Employment Opportunity Commission to ask the
National Academy of Sciences to form a committee to study the consequences of eliminating mandatory retirement for tenured faculty.  The committee was asked to conduct its study while the temporary exemption was in
effect and to report its findings to Congress prior to the expiration of the
exemption.  This is the committee's report.

The committee was well aware of the difficulty of its task.  It was asked
to assess the future effects of removing mandatory retirement not only on a
few famous schools but on more than 3,200 colleges and universities across
the United States.  These institutions include 2-year colleges, 4-year colleges, and universities.  They include those that give top priority to undergraduate teaching and those that emphasize research and the training of
future scholars, as well as specialized schools of medicine, law, business,

religion, and the arts. Some of these institutions are well endowed, some are poor, some are growing rapidly, and others barely survive.

To respond to its charge from Congress, the committee was also asked to examine the behavior, under new circumstances and at a future date, of nearly 300,000 current tenured faculty as well as an unknown number of future faculty members. This task involves complex human issues that do not admit of simple resolution.

Prior to the committee's first meeting, the staff, accompanied in some cases by the chair, conducted a series of site visits to colleges and universities to get a preliminary view of the issues. In October 1989, at the first of its seven meetings, the committee followed the instructions of Congress by hearing presentations from a number of organizations with a direct interest in policies governing mandatory retirement.

The committee's first major activity was to write to the presidents of 358 universities and colleges selected as a representative sample of institutional types. The letters were based on the committee's initial views of the issues raised by the elimination of mandatory retirement and asked for the presidents' comments on those and any other issues. The committee also sent similar letters to heads of faculty senates at the 216 colleges and universities in this group that had a faculty senate or equivalent organization. The responses to both sets of letters helped confirm our initial perceptions of the issues, provided new insights, and emphasized the variety of views held by faculty and administrators.

The committee then conducted 17 in-depth case studies of individual colleges and universities, selected to represent a range of institutional types. Staff, usually accompanied by committee members, visited each case study institution for interviews with faculty and administrators. The case study institutions also provided data on their faculty age distributions, retirement patterns, and institutional retirement policies.

The committee also reviewed available evidence in three separate broad areas of concern: faculty demographics and retirement behavior; the effects of aging on faculty performance; and financial and legal issues. In each area we reviewed evidence from researchers and practitioners on both the nature of the situation and the range of possible policy responses to any problems identified. This evidence included five commissioned papers, three workshops, literature reviews, and analyses of national faculty data bases. In some cases, we obtained evidence from individual colleges and universities rather than aggregate data. In other cases, we had faculty and administrators' accounts of their experiences rather than research results. We have used these additional sources, as well as our own years of experience as faculty, administrators, and trustees, to supplement our review of the literature and analysis of national faculty data bases.

The effects of eliminating mandatory retirement depend on the number of faculty who change their retirement behavior and the extent to which their behavior changes. Those university presidents who saw the removal of mandatory retirement as a major problem were alarmed by the prospect of large numbers of faculty deferring retirement for a number of years. They expected the continued employment of older and usually higher-salaried professors to create financial problems. They also expected difficulty maintaining the quality of their institutions if a decrease in the number of faculty retiring limited hiring and promotion of new faculty with new views and new areas of research.

A simple hypothetical example illustrates the quantitative aspect of concerns about costs and turnover. Costs could increase or turnover could decrease if allowing faculty to continue to work past age 70 leads to an increase in the average faculty retirement age. If we assume that the average career length of a faculty member is 35 years, then each year shift upward in the average age of retirement will produce an increase of a little less than 3 percent in average faculty career length and a corresponding 3 percent decrease in hiring new faculty to replace retiring faculty. This example, as well as the more sophisticated models we present in Chapter 2, indicates that several years' shift in the average retirement age would be required to make a major impact on colleges and universities and on career prospects for individual faculty members.

To assess the magnitude of potential changes in faculty retirement behavior, the committee examined data on the proportion of faculty reaching traditional retirement ages (60 and older) in the coming decades, the ages at which faculty now retire, and, more specifically, the ages at which faculty retire at colleges and universities that have already eliminated mandatory retirement. Although the last source of evidence is limited, the experiences of uncapped colleges and universities provide some direct information on faculty retirement patterns in the absence of a mandatory retirement age. The committee also examined data on changes in faculty retirement behavior that occurred when the mandatory retirement age was raised from 65 to 70 in 1982.

Studies and surveys conducted by a number of authors, notably Lozier and Dooris (1990) and Rees and Smith (1991), gave us further insight into faculty retirement behavior. Our understanding of the variance in faculty retirement behavior across institutions, as well as of faculty retirement patterns, was also enhanced by studies of faculty retirement patterns shared with us by individual universities.

Concern about the effects on research and education of eliminating mandatory retirement for tenured faculty stems partially from the belief that older faculty are less effective in the classroom or as scholars but are sheltered from dismissal by the tenure system. Some faculty and administrators expressed concern that colleges and universities would abolish the tenure system rather than allow it to shelter poorly performing faculty working past age 70. The committee developed background on this issue by holding a workshop attended by experts on the effects of aging, reviewing literature on age and performance, and commissioning a paper on the legal issues related to tenure and faculty dismissal.

Some faculty and administrators suggested that in the absence of a mandatory retirement age, colleges and universities would be obliged to rely more heavily on faculty evaluation and dismissal of older faculty whose performance was no longer adequate. Therefore, we also reviewed evidence on evaluating and dismissing tenured faculty as ways for colleges and universities to address issues of declining performance and the need for faculty turnover.

Faculty are less likely to retire if they believe their retirement incomes are inadequate, their health care costs could be prohibitive, and, in some cases, if they will lose access to colleagues, students, and institutional facilities such as library privileges, office and laboratory space, and secretarial and computer support. Faculty may also retire later if they have a retirement plan whose financial rewards rise rapidly with each year of additional service.

Therefore, the committee examined the effects of college and university retirement benefits on faculty retirement behavior. In addition to reviewing the literature on pension programs, health benefits, and other benefits for retired faculty, we commissioned a paper on legal issues in changing faculty pension policies and a paper on the costs of offering continued faculty benefits to retired faculty. We also held a workshop at which university business officers, personnel and other administrators, experts on higher education and aging, and experts on the financial and legal aspects of retirement discussed faculty retirement policies and programs. We collected additional information on the costs and effects of faculty retirement policies from individual colleges and universities, including our 17 case study institutions.

Unlike other faculty retirement policies, retirement incentive programs are specifically designed to encourage faculty turnover. Many colleges and universities already offer formal retirement incentive programs or individualized retirement incentives as a way to encourage faculty members to retire. The committee reviewed evidence on the effectiveness of retirement incentives and on the range of program designs available, including two commissioned papers reviewing the costs and legal regulations governing retirement incentive offers, literature on retirement incentive plans, additional evidence from individual colleges and universities offering retirement incentive programs and individual retirement incentives, and the discussion of experts at our workshop on the financial and legal issues of eliminating mandatory retirement.

In doing all its work, the committee has kept in mind that Congress did not ask us to rethink the rights and wrongs of mandatory retirement. Although mandatory retirement was until recently the prevailing norm, in weighing the desire of individuals to be judged for what they can do and not for their age, Congress has clearly decided against age-based retirement for almost all U.S. institutions and for almost all Americans. The committee's central task was to establish whether or not the special circumstances of tenured faculty in higher education justify an exception to this recently evolved national policy prohibiting age discrimination in employment.

The committee has prepared a report laying out its best judgment on the consequences of ending mandatory retirement in terms of faculty retirement behavior; faculty and institutional quality; and the institutional, legal, and financial issues for college and university management. We would especially call the reader's attention to a number of specific recommendations the committee makes regarding the advantages and disadvantages of different tools for maintaining faculty turnover and institutional quality. These include retirement incentive programs; pension, health, and other benefit programs; and faculty evaluation and dismissal proceedings.

The committee also makes a final recommendation regarding congressional action on the federal law that now requires elimination of mandatory retirement at the beginning of 1994.

The committee strongly urges Congress and relevant regulatory agencies, states and private pension plan providers, and individual colleges and universities to work together in solving significant problems associated with a number of retirement policies affecting faculty and institutions of higher education. These problems, and our suggestions for their solution, are detailed in this report.

Ralph E. Gomory, *Chair*
Committee on Mandatory Retirement in
Higher Education

# Acknowledgments

In the course of carrying out all of its activities, the committee benefited from the efforts of a number of groups and individuals. The Equal Employment Opportunity Commission sponsored the committee's study, and several members of its staff, including Elizabeth Thornton, Ronald Edwards, and Paul Boymel, offered their understanding at several important junctures in our work.

Seven higher education interest groups—the American Federation of Teachers, the Association of American Colleges, the Association of American Universities, the American Association of University Professors, the National Association of State and Land Grant Colleges, the American Council on Education, the National Education Association, and the American Association of Retired Persons—provided the committee with their perspectives on the consequences of ending mandatory retirement.

Administrators at 358 colleges and universities responded to our request by providing their insights in writing on key issues raised by the ADEA amendments of 1986. Faculty representatives at 216 institutions responded to a similar request.

Faculty and administrators at the 17 colleges and universities at which we conducted anonymous case studies gave us their time and extraordinary access to information about their policies, practices, data, and thoughts on faculty retirement.

The managers of national faculty data bases—the Survey of Doctoral Recipients (SDR), National Survey of Postsecondary Faculty (NSOPF), the Higher Education Research Institute survey, and the Association of American Medical Colleges faculty data bases—gave the committee demographic information and, in several cases, responded quickly to numerous requests for special tabulations. In particular, the committee appreciates the efforts of the National Research Council's Susan Mitchell and her staff.

More than 25 research universities responded to our request for data on faculty ages, including recent faculty retirements. This allowed the committee to examine, for these institutions, the proportion of faculty retiring at age 70 and, for the small number of uncapped research institutions, the number and proportion of faculty over age 70. In many cases, providing these data involved considerable time and effort of the university's staff.

The committee also wishes to recognize the contributions of the staff of the National Research Council. As study codirector, Pamela Ebert Flattau helped the committee initiate its activities, including organizing a workshop and a survey of the literature on aging performance. Later, after her appointment in the spring of 1990 as director of the NRC division that conducts and analyzes the SDR, Dr. Flattau assisted us in our use of those data. Dorothy Gilford, senior technical adviser to the committee, was instrumental in developing an initial conceptualization of the study. She also designed and managed the committee's letters of inquiry and made initial data requests. Gary Selnow contributed significantly to the committee's work in developing, evaluating, and presenting sources of data on faculty ages and retirement behavior. Suellen Crano organized the committee's campus case studies and campus-level data gathering. She also contributed substantively to other staff activities, including analysis of research on aging and performance. Ellen Tenenbaum prepared summaries of responses to letters of inquiry and assisted in tabulating data on faculty demographics. Eugenia Grohman provided able assistance in editing and guiding the committee's report throughout the publication process. Gale Moore, Joe Masteika, Jane Phillips, and, especially, Carol Palma, provided continuity and an extraordinary level of administrative support for all of the committee's varied activities.

Harriet Morgan initially contributed to the committee's analysis of legal and financial issues associated with faculty retirement. Subsequently, she undertook major writing responsibilities, working closely with the study director and the committee in crafting the report.

Finally, the committee notes its special debt to Brett Hammond for his thoughtful stewardship of the study. His able direction of the staff and his assistance from study design to research to creating the final report helped to bring order and reason to the wide range of activities the committee undertook.

# Executive Summary

In 1986 the U.S. Congress passed legislation amending the Age Discrimination in Employment Act (ADEA) of 1967 to prohibit mandatory retirement on the basis of age for almost all workers. The amendments included an exemption, which terminates at the end of 1993, permitting mandatory retirement of any employee who is serving under a contract of unlimited tenure at an institution of higher education and who has attained 70 years of age (ADEA, 1986, Section 12(d)).

In granting this exemption, Congress took a middle position between those who wished to extend full protection against age discrimination to faculty and those who feared that postponed faculty retirements would prevent colleges and universities from hiring new faculty, who are traditionally a source of new ideas. Some people were also concerned that an aging professoriate would grow increasingly ineffective but unremovable because of the tenure system. Administrators, faculty, policy makers, and others who recognize the importance of the nation's basic research system were particularly concerned about possible adverse effects on the research universities.

As a part of the 1986 amendments, Congress directed the Equal Employment Opportunity Commission to ask the National Academy of Sciences to conduct a study analyzing "the potential consequences of the elimination of mandatory retirement in institutions of higher education" (ADEA, 1986, Section 12(c)). The committee's central task—the subject of this report—is to establish whether the special circumstances of tenured faculty in higher education justify a continued exception to the national policy prohibiting age discrimination in employment. The task was complicated by its scope: to assess the effects of removing mandatory retirement on more than 3,200 colleges and universities and to assess the behavior, under

*1*

new circumstances and at a future date, of nearly 300,000 current tenured faculty as well as an unknown number of future faculty members. It was further complicated by the need to evaluate the effects of something that had not yet occurred, since most of the states that have eliminated mandatory retirement have done so within the past few years.

Although the committee could not avoid the exercise of its judgment in a matter of this complexity, it based that judgment on all the available relevant data it could obtain. The committee reviewed current faculty retirement patterns as well as studies projecting future patterns. The committee also examined college and university tenure, evaluation, and retirement policies. Institutional policies affect faculty retirement patterns, and changes in those policies could provide a basis for responding to the elimination of mandatory retirement. Thus, in order to estimate the costs and benefits of the potential elimination of mandatory retirement, the committee considered whether policies—both institutional and congressional—exist that would mitigate the potential adverse effects of uncapping.

We base two key conclusions on our review of the evidence:

• **At most colleges and universities, few tenured faculty would continue working past age 70 if mandatory retirement is eliminated.** Most faculty retire before age 70. The few uncapped colleges and universities with data report that the proportion of faculty over age 70 is no more than 1.6 percent.

• **At some research universities, a high proportion of faculty would choose to work past age 70 if mandatory retirement is eliminated.** At a small number of research universities, more than 40 percent of the faculty who retire each year have done so at the current mandatory retirement age of 70. Evidence suggests that faculty who are research oriented, enjoy inspiring students, have light teaching loads, and are covered by pension plans that reward later retirement are more likely to work past age 70.

These two conclusions underlie the rest of our conclusions and our recommendations. If mandatory retirement is eliminated, **some research universities are likely to suffer adverse effects** from low faculty turnover: increased costs and limited flexibility to respond to changing needs and to provide support for new fields by hiring new faculty.

An increase in the number of faculty over age 70 or, more generally, an increase in the average age of faculty does not by itself, as distinct from reduced turnover, affect institutional quality. Available evidence does not show significant declines in faculty performance caused by age.

At most colleges and universities, few faculty are likely to work past age 70. **Therefore, eliminating mandatory retirement would not pose a**

**threat to tenure.** Colleges and universities can dismiss tenured faculty, provided they afford due process in a clearly defined and understood dismissal procedure, with the burden of proving cause resting with the institution; however, dismissal of faculty members for poor performance is rare now and likely to remain rare.

In response to larger concerns about faculty performance, the committee recommends that faculty and administrators work to develop ways to offer faculty feedback on their performance. Colleges and universities hoping to hire scholars in new fields or to change the balance of faculty research and teaching interests will need to encourage turnover using mechanisms other than performance evaluation and dismissal.

**Retirement incentive programs are clearly an important tool for increasing turnover.** They should be considered by any college or university concerned about the effects of faculty working past age 70, including reduced faculty turnover and increased costs. Colleges and universities can target such programs to fields or disciplines in which turnover is most needed, and they can limit participation to control both turnover and costs.

The committee emphasizes that retirement incentive programs and individual retirement incentive contracts must be entered into freely and without coercion, when seen by both the institution and the individual as beneficial. The committee recommends that colleges and universities offer retirement incentive programs and individual retirement incentive contracts only to tenured faculty aged 50 and over. Retirement incentive programs now used in higher education are commonly designed for faculty in their 60s. By extending participation in these programs to faculty aged 50 and over, colleges and universities could benefit by increasing faculty turnover and in planning for faculty retirements.

Congress has clearly authorized retirement incentive programs that include a minimum age for participation, that are offered for a window of time, and that provide bridge payments until retirees are eligible for Social Security benefits. Congress and the responsible federal agencies could assist colleges and universities further by clearly preserving additional options.

**The committee recommends that Congress, the Internal Revenue Service, and the Equal Employment Opportunity Commission also permit colleges and universities to offer faculty voluntary retirement incentive programs that: are not classified as an employee benefit, include an upper age limit for participants, and limit participation on the basis of institutional needs.**

We believe that financial concerns should not be pivotal in faculty retirement decisions. **Faculty pension, health insurance, and other retirement policies should create neither disincentives to retirement nor inadvertent incentives to postpone retirement.**

Therefore, we recommend that:

 • colleges and universities offer pension plans designed to provide retired faculty with a continuing retirement income from all sources equal to between 67 and 100 percent of their preretirement income;
 • TIAA-CREF, other private pension plan providers, and state retirement systems work with institutions of higher education to develop pension plans that provide continuing retirement incomes within the committee's suggested range; and
 • Congress, the Internal Revenue Service, and the Equal Employment Opportunity Commission adopt policies allowing employers to limit contributions to defined contribution plans on the basis of estimated level of pension income.

We suggest a maximum as well as a minimum goal for inflation-protected pension income in the interest of best allocating scarce resources and limiting inadvertent incentives to postpone retirement. If colleges and universities save any funds by limiting institutional pension contributions, they can redirect them to other benefits for retired faculty, such as health benefits and programs for retirees.

Inadequate or expensive retirement health coverage creates a disincentive to retirement. We recommend that administrators and faculty seek affordable ways to improve retirees' medical coverage, such as redirecting funds from other retirement benefit programs or establishing tax-sheltered health savings plans for faculty to save for their own retirement health costs.

Faculty members who are considering retirement may be reluctant to give up regular contact with students and colleagues or such faculty privileges as access to a laboratory or library. We recommend that colleges and universities seek opportunities for retired faculty to maintain their contacts with colleagues, the institution, and their field of scholarship. Retirement planning assistance also can ease the transition to retirement and make retirement a more attractive option. The committee recommends that all colleges and universities assist their faculty in planning for retirement.

## The ADEA Exemption

The committee believes that if colleges and universities, with assistance from Congress and regulatory agencies, states, and pension plan providers, vigorously pursue these recommendations, all but a few institutions will adjust to the elimination of mandatory retirement without significant effects. The few universities at which a high proportion of faculty members are most likely to work past age 70 will particularly need the congressional and regulatory actions we recommend: clarifying retirement incentive options and revising pension policies.

The committee also believes that some aspects of eliminating mandatory retirement are clearly beneficial. Most obviously, faculty gain freedom in deciding when to retire. Eliminating mandatory retirement would be in keeping with the general intent of the ADEA to extend protection against age discrimination.

In this report the committee has examined a number of practical steps that are available or could be made available to address the problems raised by the elimination of mandatory retirement.

**The committee recommends that Congress and regulatory agencies, states and pension plan providers, and colleges and universities take these practical steps.**

**Given that these steps can be taken, there is no strong basis for continuing the exemption for tenured faculty.**

**The committee recommends that the ADEA exemption permitting the mandatory retirement of tenured faculty be allowed to expire at the end of 1993.**

# 1

# Introduction: Faculty Retirement and Age Discrimination

In the closing hours of the 1986 congressional session, the House and Senate reached agreement on legislation amending the Age Discrimination in Employment Act (ADEA) of 1967 to prohibit mandatory retirement on the basis of age for all workers except for tenured faculty in higher education, police officers, fire fighters, and a few executives and high-level policy makers. The exemption for tenured faculty, which terminates at the end of 1993, permits mandatory retirement of any employee who is serving under a contract of unlimited tenure at an institution of higher education and who has attained 70 years of age (ADEA, 1986, Section 12(d)).

In granting a temporary exemption for tenured faculty, Congress took a middle position between those who wished to extend full protection against age discrimination to faculty and those who feared that postponed faculty retirements would prevent colleges and universities from hiring new faculty, who are traditionally a source of new ideas. Some were also concerned that an aging professoriate would grow increasingly ineffective but unremovable because of the tenure system. Limited opportunities for hiring or an ineffective professoriate could adversely affect the quality of research and teaching in the nation's colleges and universities. Administrators, faculty, policy makers, and others who recognize the importance of the nation's basic research system were particularly concerned about possible negative effects on the research universities.

As a part of the compromise, Congress directed the Equal Employment Opportunity Commission to ask the National Academy of Sciences (NAS) to conduct a study analyzing "the potential consequences of the elimination of mandatory retirement in institutions of higher education" (ADEA, 1986, Section 12(c)). The committee's central task—the subject of this report—is to establish whether the special circumstances of tenured faculty in higher education justify a continued exception to the national policy prohibiting age discrimination in employment.

In the first part of this chapter we examine the origin of the tenured faculty exemption as part of the evolution of federal policy against age discrimination. In the second part we delineate the main issues raised by the possibility of eliminating mandatory retirement for tenured faculty and indicate where they are presented in depth in the rest of the report.

## TENURE AND THE FACULTY EXEMPTION

### Tenure in Higher Education

The issue of the tenured faculty exemption focused on the special characteristics of tenure in higher education. Tenure in U.S. colleges and universities arose in the latter half of the nineteenth century, largely as a protection for faculty against dismissal for exercising freedom of speech and inquiry. The 1940 Statement of Principles on Academic Freedom and Tenure developed by the American Association of University Professors and the Association of American Colleges, generally regarded as the "standard" for academic tenure (see Commission on Academic Tenure in Higher Education, 1973:1), provides that after a fixed probationary period, a faculty member should be considered carefully by peers and academic administrators for tenure on the basis of his or her accomplishments in teaching, scholarship, and college or university service. A college or university may offer tenure immediately to new faculty who have made contributions while employed at other colleges and universities. The 1940 statement (American Association of University Professors, 1990:4) declares that a tenured faculty member "should be terminated only for adequate cause, except in cases of retirement for age or under extraordinary circumstances because of financial exigencies."

The concept of tenure is not unique to higher education. For example, most precollege public education in the United States is carried out by teachers who receive tenure after a 1- to 3-year probationary period. Other government workers also usually have security of employment, often labeled tenure. Even some private companies give additional protection against layoffs to employees with long service.

What sets tenure in higher education apart is the emphasis on job security in order to preserve intellectual freedom. Congress recognized that the special nature of the tenure contract could create special issues for legislation affecting employment in higher education.

Although there is nothing in the congressional committee report explaining the exemption for tenured faculty or the request for an independent study, Senate debate on the ADEA amendments noted the potential for conflict between age discrimination policy and certain higher education interests (*Congressional Record*, October 16, 1986:S16852-S16856):

> Mr. Metzenbaum: . . . At present, the case for a permanent exemption [of public safety employees and tenured faculty] has not been made. I, for one, am not certain that such a case can be made.
>
> Mr. Heinz: . . . Special concerns about . . . the tenure system at colleges and universities have been raised.
>
> Mr. Moynihan: . . . I must note, however, that I am troubled by the application of this change to the unique situation of tenured faculty members at colleges and universities. In order for these institutions to remain effective centers of teaching and scholarship, they must have a balance of old and new faculty. Hence, universities must ensure that older faculty members retire at an appropriate age, not simply to "make room" for younger faculty, but to maintain a contemporary, innovative and creative atmosphere where students can obtain the fullest education. . . . Unfortunately, I am not at all certain that this bill adequately takes into account the history of academia since the late 1950's. As a result of vast expansion in the number of individuals pursuing careers in academia at this time, there is now a bulge of faculty members who will not be retiring before the end of this century— even if they retire at the current mandatory age of 70. This is certainly not to criticize in any way these undoubtedly qualified faculty members. But there does appear to be a severe shortage of teaching positions available for today's scholars. And the situation at this time is such that most new faculty openings occur as a result of retirement. We should be very careful, I think, about eliminating the retirement age altogether, unless we can be sure that the Nation's education will not suffer as a result.
>
> Therefore, I note that the legislation before us today provides a temporary exemption, for 7 years, of tenured faculty. . . . I would have preferred an even longer period—12 or 15 years—but note that the House inexplicably chose not to provide any exemption.
>
> Importantly, during the 7-year period, the bill calls upon the NAS to appoint . . . a nine member Commission to study the impact of the change. . . . This study will be due in 5 years, allowing the Congress to adequately review the effects of this bill on academic committees, and make the appropriate changes in order to protect the vital national resource embodied in education.
>
> Mr. Hatch: . . . This bill contains an effective compromise involving public safety officials and tenured university faculty . . . [T]his [NAS] report . . . will help determine whether further amendments will be necessary in order to maintain the delicate balance between the right of every individual to be judged on the basis of his or her skill and experience and the interests of the general public. . . .

Efforts to accommodate antidiscrimination policies with the interests of higher education did not begin with passage of the 1986 amendments. Since the early 1960s, the federal government had taken a series of steps to extend protection against age discrimination to workers in an increasing number of employment sectors. At the same time, Congress made repeated exceptions to this general trend in response to concerns that abolishing mandatory retirement for tenured professors could harm higher education.

## Age Discrimination in Employment Act and Its Amendments

Federal action to remove the mandatory retirement age for tenured faculty began with the 1961 White House Conference on Aging (1961:155), which recommended "steps to prevent mandatory, compulsory retirement at an arbitrary age" for all workers. In 1967, after several years in which legislation embodying this principle was introduced in Congress but not passed, President Lyndon Johnson proposed and Congress passed the Age Discrimination in Employment Act, protecting some private-sector workers from discrimination in hiring and retirement practices.

The 1967 act made age discrimination illegal. According to historical accounts, it drew little attention from the higher education community or from most other major employee and employer groups, perhaps because it (1) set 65 as the minimum mandatory retirement age, thereby adopting what was common practice in higher education and many other sectors; (2) did not cover employees at public institutions; and (3) allowed private institutions that provide an employee pension plan meeting certain Internal Revenue Service (IRS) standards to require retirement before age 65 (see Pratt, 1989:15-19).

Largely in response to the efforts of the American Association of Retired Persons (AARP) and the National Retired Teachers Association (NRTA), Congress extended ADEA protection in 1974 to cover employees of state and federal governments and in 1975 to cover employees of all federally assisted organizations—including most private colleges and universities (Pratt, 1989:17). The amendments did not eliminate the exemption for institutions with qualified pension plans, and they also retained 65 as the allowable mandatory retirement age.

In 1977, with active support from the AARP and the NRTA, Representative Claude Pepper proposed legislation that would:

• raise the minimum mandatory retirement age to 70 for private-sector, state, and local government workers;

• eliminate the mandatory retirement age for federal workers; and

• eliminate the exemption in the original act that allows mandatory retirement before age 65 for employees covered by an IRS-qualified pension plan.

A bill embodying these elements moved swiftly through Congress. Near the end of the legislative process, higher education groups developed a variety of positions on the proposed changes. Some groups advised their members to support a permanent or temporary exemption for faculty members on the grounds that academic tenure is different from employment practices in businesses and other organizations subject to the proposed changes in the ADEA (Pratt, 1989:21). In contrast, other groups supported mandatory retirement in principle as a way to ensure a continuing stream of job openings for all workers and rejected granting special status on the matter to higher education. Most higher education groups based their positions on one or more of the following justifications:

1. The high proportion of tenured faculty, owing to the large number of faculty hired in the 1950s and 1960s, would be increased further by legislation allowing continued employment until age 70.

2. An undersupply of job openings for able young faculty would be further reduced as older faculty members continued to work.

3. The limited number of job openings would also stymie affirmative action on behalf of minorities and women.

4. Many academic administrators and faculty feared that "uncapping" would lead to more frequent and costly performance evaluations and to dismissal of tenured professors, thereby threatening faculty tenure protections.

According to Pratt (1989), members of Congress, including those with experience in higher education such as Senators Daniel Moynihan and S. I. Hayakawa, were most concerned by the first and fourth points. Based on these arguments, Senator John Chafee submitted an amendment to the bill that would permit colleges and universities to maintain mandatory retirement at age 65 for tenured faculty.

Senate debate on the bill in the fall of 1977 focused entirely on the proposed faculty exemption, sounding significant themes that would arise again in connection with the 1986 ADEA amendments. Some Senators invoked civil rights as a basis for rejecting the special exemption for faculty; other Senators supported the exemption on the grounds that it would provide continued employment opportunities for younger faculty and that it would obviate the difficult task of developing improved performance evaluation procedures in higher education. Although the Senate ultimately adopted the Chafee amendment, the House and Senate conference committee decided to make the exemption for higher education temporary, expiring July 1, 1982.

Congress also responded to more widespread concern about the impact that changing mandatory retirement rules "would have on the ability of employers to assure promotional opportunities for younger workers" (U.S. Senate, 1978:510) On the grounds that private firms and other organizations benefit from regular turnover in top leadership positions, Congress accepted Senator Claiborne Pell's proposed amendment to create a permanent exemption permitting mandatory retirement at age 65 for highly compensated executives and high-level policy makers who are eligible for at least $44,000 in annual pension income (ADEA, 1986, Section 12(c)(1)). Congress and the courts have restricted this exemption to an extremely small number of positions in an organization.

Raising the mandatory retirement "cap" from 65 to 70 represented a significant change for higher education. At that time two-thirds of the tenured faculty in the United States were employed at colleges and universities with a mandatory retirement age of less than 70 (Holden and Hansen, 1989:36). Between the bill's passage in 1978 and the end of the temporary exemption in 1982, a number of states and individual colleges and universities raised their mandatory retirement ages from 65 to 70. By 1982 there was little impetus for continuing the age 65 cap, and the exemption was allowed to lapse.

Following passage of the 1978 amendments, Representative Claude Pepper and various groups continued to lobby for complete elimination of mandatory retirement for all employees in United States, including tenured faculty. Pepper and Senator John Heinz submitted bills embodying this objective in 1982 and again in 1984, but serious support for further amending the ADEA came in 1985, largely from public-safety officers and the U.S. Chamber of Commerce (Pratt, 1989:26). These two groups, along with groups representing older Americans principally, the AARP and teachers (the American Federation of Teachers [AFT] and the National Education Association [NEA]), urged Pepper and Heinz to resubmit their legislation eliminating the mandatory retirement.

Once again, a number of education groups opposed the legislation. They raised concerns that the large number of faculty hired in the 1960s would not reach retirement age until the late 1990s and that any significant increase in retirement age in this group would diminish the number of openings in academia for younger scholars. Other education groups opposed the legislation because they believed that opportunities for all younger workers, not only professors, would be affected by uncapping.

Given the disparity of views among higher education groups and other special interest groups, as well as Pepper's strong advocacy for extending civil rights to all Americans over age 70, Congress ended mandatory retirement but granted temporary exemptions—until January 1, 1994—for tenured professors, fire fighters, and police officers. The 1986 amendments also retained the permanent exemptions for highly compensated executives and high-level policy makers.

After the passage of the 1986 amendments, some higher education groups, college and university administrators, and faculty expressed alarm at the prospect of a significant number of faculty deferring retirement, possibly for many years. They continued to raise concerns about decreased opportunities for younger faculty and about possible threats to tenure. They also warned of a loss of collegiality likely to result from increased attempts to identify and dismiss nonperforming faculty and of the increased cost of salaries and benefits or retirement incentive programs for higher numbers of senior faculty members (Heller, 1986; Mangan, 1987). A small number of groups and individuals suggested that problems might be more acute at some or all research universities, which face high scientific and medical research costs and have low faculty turnover.

## THE COMMITTEE'S STUDY:  SCOPE AND ISSUES

Traditionally, tenure in higher education has offered employment security until a mandatory retirement age, and most colleges and universities have had the choice of allowing individual faculty members to stay beyond that age. The elimination of mandatory retirement transfers that choice from colleges and universities to individual faculty members. Therefore, individual faculty members would gain additional options in choosing a retirement age if mandatory retirement were eliminated.

Although there is much to be said on both sides of the issue, the Committee on Mandatory Retirement in Higher Education was not asked to rethink the rights and wrongs of age-based retirement, which until recently was the prevailing norm. One can argue that mandatory retirement is an impersonal, dignified way to end employment without having to prove deficient performance and that an institution's need for new people can often be considered more important than an individual's desire for a few more years of employment. In weighing these factors against the desire of individuals to be judged for what they can do, not for their age, Congress has clearly decided against age-based retirement for almost all U.S. institutions and for almost all Americans.

In a few instances, Congress has recognized special circumstances, such as the permanent exemption retaining mandatory retirement for a small number of highly compensated executives and high-level policy makers (ADEA, Section 12(c)(1)). The committee's central task was to establish whether or not the special circumstances of tenured faculty in higher education justify an exception to the national policy prohibiting age discrimination in employment.

The committee's task was complicated by its scope. We were asked to assess the effects of removing mandatory retirement, not with respect to faculty at few colleges and universities with similar characteristics, but with respect to faculty at some 3,200 institutions across the United States. These institutions range from those that emphasize undergraduate teaching to those that stress research and the training of future scholars; from community colleges to a large array of schools of engineering, medicine, law, religion, and other specialized subjects. Some of these institutions are well endowed, and some are poor; some are growing rapidly, and some are barely surviving. Thus, the employment conditions of faculty vary widely, even at institutions of similar purpose, depending on the institution's financial conditions, whether it is public or private, and other factors.

The committee's task was complicated further by the need to evaluate the effects of something that had not yet occurred. There are few opportunities to study faculty retirement behavior and institutional responses in the absence of mandatory retirement. Most of the states that have eliminated mandatory retirement have done so within the past few years, so there is little experience to observe. Turning to possible cross-national comparisons, there is also little to draw on because most countries have legislatively or administratively defined a mandatory retirement age: for example, the Soviet Union recently imposed a mandatory retirement age for some scientists, and Canada's highest court recently ruled that higher education in that country is still subject to mandatory retirement. Therefore, the committee was being asked to assess the behavior, under new circumstances and at a future date, of nearly 300,000 current tenured faculty as well as an unknown number of future faculty members. In sum, the committee's task involves complex human issues that do not admit of simple resolution.

## The Committee's Activities

Although the committee could not avoid the exercise of its judgment in a matter of this complexity, we were determined to base such judgment on as much relevant data as we could obtain. The committee thus carried out a variety of activities in addition to its regular meetings and discussions (see Appendix A for a complete description of the committee's data-gathering and analysis activities).

• We invited groups interested in higher education retirement policy to provide their views and insights to the committee. The groups were those named by Congress in mandating the committee's study: the Association of American Universities, the American Council on Education, and the National Association of State Universities and Land Grant Colleges, which represent colleges and universities; the American Association of University Professors, the American Federation of Teachers and the National Education Association, which represent faculty; and the American Association of Retired Persons.

• As a way of obtaining a range of institutional and faculty views on the issues, the committee wrote to the presidents and heads of faculty senates of 358 colleges and universities selected as a representative sample of the various types of higher education institutions (216 of the sample institutions had a faculty senate or equivalent organization). The letter asked for their anonymous comments on a list of issues pertaining to mandatory retirement in higher education and invited institutions to raise any other relevant issues. Both sets of letters produced much confirming material and some fresh insight into the nature of the problem, and they provided a sweep of the views represented by the various institutions and their faculties.

• We conducted 17 in-depth case studies of individual institutions in order to understand the context in which faculty make retirement decisions and institutions set policies affecting those decisions. Although 17 institutions cannot represent all U.S. colleges and universities, the committee's cases represented a range of colleges and universities. These studies included extensive discussions with faculty and administrators.

• The committee sponsored three workshops involving presentations by knowledgeable and interested individuals and groups, commissioned five papers by experts in specific fields, and reviewed literature, including recently completed and ongoing studies of faculty retirement behavior, in order to marshall all available findings and information relevant to faculty retirement issues.

• The committee collected retirement data for the past 5-10 years from selected institutions, including all of our case study colleges and universities, supplemented by special requests to other institutions. We also examined the major national faculty data bases maintained by the U.S. Department of Education, the Higher Education Research Institute, and the National Research Council.

These activities, as well as our seven meetings over a period of 15 months, enabled the committee to develop a set of issues and questions particularly relevant to understanding the effects of uncapping. Committee members also drew on their extensive experience as faculty, administrators, and trustees at a broad range of colleges and universities.

## Issues and Report Structure

### Faculty Retirement Behavior and Turnover

*How many tenured faculty are likely to continue working past age 70 if given the chance?* In Chapter 2 we examine the pivotal question of how much the behavior of faculty would change as a result of uncapping. Administrators and faculty members responding to our letters and in case study interviews were concerned that paying higher-salaried professors for longer periods of time could create financial problems and that a generally older faculty and lower hiring rates for new faculty could threaten the vitality of teaching and research at their institutions.

A simple hypothetical case illustrates concerns about costs and turnover. Costs could increase and turnover could decrease if allowing faculty to continue to work past age 70 leads to an increase in the average faculty retirement age. An increase in faculty working past age 70 balanced by increased retirements at earlier ages would have less effect. For example, assume that the average length of service for a faculty member is roughly 35 years and that a college or university generally can hire new faculty only when a position becomes vacant through retirement (i.e., institutions cannot afford to increase the size of the faculty). Under these circumstances, if the length of professorial service rose by 1 year to 36 years, an increase of a little less than 3 percent, there would be a corresponding 3 percent decrease in the number of positions opening up for new faculty. If the institution continued to hire (i.e., increased faculty size) then salary, benefit, and support costs for faculty would rise. This simplified model leaves out transition effects and the relatively higher cost of older faculty members, but it indicates the relationship between a shift in average retirement age and an institution's ability to hire. Colleges and universities hire new faculty as a way to bring in new ideas and research specialties. Some institutions that want to remain current in research fields believe they could be adversely affected by later faculty retirements and the resulting lower turnover.

Two other perceived demographic issues in higher education could interact with the potential effects of eliminating mandatory retirement. A number of respondents to our letter inquiry mentioned a possible faculty age "bulge" created by increased faculty hiring in response to student enrollment growth from the late 1950s through the early 1970s. One issue is the possible existence of disproportionate numbers of faculty at certain ages, either overall or by type of institution or discipline, as well as what effect, if any, this might have on faculty retirement behavior. Another issue is a possible faculty shortage arising during the next 15 years as the number of new Ph.D.s fails to keep pace with projected increases in student enrollments and eventual faculty retirements (Bowen and Sosa, 1989; Atkinson, 1990).

To address these issues, in Chapter 2 we examine data on the current national faculty age structure and changes in age distribution over time, as well as projections of faculty supply and demand and the implications for faculty retirement behavior and policies. We also review data and studies that compare recent faculty retirement behavior at states and institutions that have already eliminated mandatory retirement and on changes in national faculty retirement behavior in response to the retirement age between 1978 and 1982.

*How might faculty retirement patterns vary among different fields and colleges and universities?* Faculty could be more likely to continue working past age 70 in certain fields or at certain types of institutions. Hence, the effects of eliminating mandatory retirement could be more severe in these fields and at those institutions. Administrators and faculty at research universities, in particular, expressed concern in their letters and in discussions during site visits and case studies that faculty at their universities would work past age 70 and that this could pose severe problems for the institution. In order to estimate potential variations in faculty retirement behavior if mandatory retirement were eliminated, in Chapter 2 we examine faculty retirement data disaggregated by type of institution and field. We also evaluate research studies of factors—such as quality of students, research emphasis, and generosity of retirement programs—that could explain any observed differences. Finally, in order to examine the effects of increases in faculty retirement ages on faculty hiring and salary costs, we adapt several models designed to simulate faculty turnover, hiring, and costs with faculty age and retirement data from a few institutions.

## Tenure, Performance Evaluation, and Aging

*How would increased numbers of faculty over age 70 affect the quality of teaching and research?* Estimates of the proportion of faculty likely to continue working past age 70 provide information as to whether older faculty will be present in colleges and universities, but they do not provide a basis for determining whether that presence is harmful or helpful to colleagues and to institutions. In Chapter 3 we address concerns about the impact of ending mandatory retirement on research, teaching, and service in higher education. In their responses to the committee's letters, administrators and faculty expressed considerable fear that faculty working into their eighth decade could suffer declines in performance that would lower the quality of some colleges and universities and the overall quality of higher education. Administrators and faculty members at research universities were particularly concerned about the effects on basic research of an increase in the proportion of older faculty members. The committee reviews available data on the relationship between performance and aging in higher education, including studies of aging and teaching and research effectiveness.

*What are the implications for tenure?* In Chapter 3 we also examine whether tenure could shelter incompetent professors from dismissal proceedings or from attempts to improve faculty performance. Faculty and administrators, in response to our letters and in our case study discussions, indicated that they have looked to mandatory retirement as a way of removing colleagues whose performance no longer meets institutional standards. Some of them believe that ending mandatory retirement would threaten tenure through pressure on institutions to identify and remove declining performers among the faculty who can no longer be expected to retire by a fixed date. Some even proposed abolishing tenure altogether in response to ending mandatory retirement (see Mangan, 1987:A13). The committee carefully considers the relationship between tenure and mandatory retirement, including questions of dismissal and performance evaluation.

*Would colleges and universities need to reassess the use of performance evaluation in response to the end of mandatory retirement?* A number of observers have proposed strengthening faculty performance evaluation or making its use more widespread in response to ending mandatory retirement. Improving the performance of or weeding out nonperforming faculty, if it can be done, is something that has always been desirable, with or without the age cap and irrespective of the age of any faculty member. The question for performance evaluation, as for tenure, is how far it is possible to change existing practices while still maintaining the collegial nature of academic institutions and the individual academic freedom of faculty. In Chapter 3 we evaluate the literature on performance evaluation in higher education and other sectors, including approaches to performance evaluation and uses of performance evaluation to maintain or improve faculty and institutional quality.

## Financial and Other Factors Affecting Retirement

*How can faculty retirement policies help institutions and individuals meet the consequences of eliminating removing the mandatory retirement?* The committee reviewed college and university retirement policies as well as current faculty retirement patterns. We believe that institutional policies affect faculty retirement patterns, and changes in those policies could provide a basis for responding to the elimination of mandatory retirement. Thus, we cannot estimate the costs and benefits of the potential elimination of mandatory retirement without considering whether policies—both institutional and congressional—exist that would mitigate the potential adverse effects of uncapping. Institutions may need to change a range of policies that affect individual retirement decisions. People are not as likely to retire if they are financially unable to do so, if they fear inflation or overwhelming medical expenses, or if they can gain financially by not retiring. Both faculty and administrators worry that some pension, tax, and other financial policies either create disincentives to retirement or reward faculty who postpone retirement.

In Chapter 4 the committee analyzes programs and policies that influence faculty retirement behavior. We examine the effectiveness of pension systems, health insurance, retirement planning assistance, and institutional planning and cost-effective ways to improve retirement policies and change the pattern of rewards and disincentives in individual retirement decisions.

*What other factors affect retirement decisions?* There are dimensions to the question of retirement other than financial issues. Many older faculty wish to continue some level of engagement with their subject matter or with their colleagues or students. Some want part-time employment, the continued use of office or laboratory space, or secretarial or computer support. In Chapter 4 we explore the range of possible activities for retired or partially retired faculty, their attractiveness, and their costs.

## Retirement Incentive Programs

*How can colleges and universities continue hiring new faculty and supporting new fields?* In Chapter 5 the committee focuses on voluntary retirement incentive programs as a mechanism specifically designed to encourage faculty turnover. We consider the range of programs that colleges and universities, states, and the federal government might use to enable institutions to hire more new faculty if mandatory retirement is eliminated. We consider the cost of retirement incentive programs used in higher education, the legal issues of offering retirement incentives, and the literature on retirement incentive programs, and we make recommendations for colleges and universities considering such programs. We also note ways in which Congress could assist colleges and universities that want to use voluntary retirement incentive programs as a way of increasing both faculty turnover and the ability to hire new faculty.

## Eliminating Mandatory Retirement

Lastly, in Chapter 6 the committee summarizes its major conclusions about the potential impact of eliminating mandatory retirement for tenured faculty. On the basis of these conclusions, the committee makes its recommendation to Congress on whether to retain the special exemption in ADEA for higher education. The committee also offers recommendations to Congress, to institutions of higher education, to pension and insurance plan providers, and to faculty on specific policies that can help to maintain and improve the quality of basic research and teaching in higher education while protecting the rights of older workers.

# 2

# Effects of Uncapping
# on Faculty Retirement

The higher education groups who favored an exemption from ADEA were concerned that many tenured faculty would choose to work well into their eighth decade if permitted to do so. They were also worried that delayed retirements might lead to low faculty turnover. One administrator responded to our letter: "While no institution wishes to lose talented faculty, turnover through retirement . . . does allow for the infusion of new ideas and energy into an institution." Another recognized that a faculty member rarely switches fields, so that retirements create opportunities for colleges and universities to reallocate positions across departments:

> It is increasingly the case that departures result in recruiting in departments other than those in which the vacancies occur. . . . A lower rate of faculty turnover implies that resources will become available at a slower rate to move to new subject areas and to areas that require additional resources.

In order to address these concerns, three questions are central to analysis of the effects of uncapping on faculty and on colleges and universities.

1. *Would some faculty would work past the current mandatory retirement age of 70 if they could?* Since most colleges and universities now require tenured faculty to retire at 70, we examined historical information about faculty demographics and retirement behavior, supplemented by data from a few colleges and universities that have recently eliminated mandatory retirement. In answering these questions, we evaluated data on the number of faculty nearing retirement age (approximately 60-70 years) in the next few years and evidence pertaining to the proportion of this group likely to postpone retirement past age 70.

2. *Are faculty in some types of colleges or universities more likely to continue working into their 70s if permitted to do so? How would this*

*affect average retirement ages at those institutions?* Some administrators and faculty reported that at certain institutions, such as the research universities, faculty are more likely to continue working past age 70. We evaluated evidence on faculty age structure and retirement patterns in a variety of institutions.

3. *What would the major effects be on colleges, universities, and higher education, in general, if faculty worked past age 70?* Many faculty and administrators believe that to stay in the forefront of scholarship it is important to hire new faculty. As McPherson and Winston (1988:183) note:

> An important aspect of the technology of university production, the result of the specialized human capital possessed by academics, is that it is rarely as easy to substitute employees among jobs as it is to hire new employees from outside for those particular jobs.

For example, a historian is unlikely to be a productive teacher and researcher in particle physics. At universities emphasizing research, specialization may be of even greater importance: An elementary particle physicist is unlikely to switch specialties easily or rapidly to high-temperature superconductivity. In some areas, however, faculty skills may be broader: Some introductory science courses could be taught by faculty in related disciplines. The degree of institutional change resulting from a retirement followed by a new hire depends on whether institutional policy allows departments to refill vacated positions or whether openings are transferred across departments. However, at both the departmental and the institutional level, turnover creates opportunities to bring in new faculty.

A rise in the average retirement age for current tenured faculty would reduce turnover, thereby limiting the number of tenure or tenure-track positions available for new faculty. Such a rise could be caused by an increase in the number of faculty working past age 70 after the elimination of mandatory retirement or by a large number of faculty retiring later than they do now, even if few or none waited until after age 70. We projected the potential effects of postponed retirements on colleges' and universities' resources, including their budgets and ability to hire new faculty. We also considered how our findings on these issues might be related to other research that projects a disproportionate number of future faculty retirements in certain age groups and the possibility of a future nationwide faculty shortage.

In addressing the above questions, we drew on a number of studies, sparked by the 1977 and 1986 changes in the ADEA, that analyzed faculty retirement behavior. We also considered information from national faculty data bases as a check on published faculty age structures and trends. We used information from the committee's letter of inquiry and case studies to identify potential problem areas and to illustrate the findings and conclusions suggested by more systematic studies. Finally, we obtained data on recent retirement patterns from some universities at which our research suggested high proportions of faculty might work past age 70 if mandatory retirement were eliminated.

In piecing together this mosaic of existing research and data, the committee found a reasonable basis for making certain inferences about retirement patterns over the coming decade. In this chapter we report our findings on faculty demographics and retirement behavior for higher education as a whole. We also examine the evidence for claims of more severe effects on faculty hiring and budgets at some universities and in some disciplines.

## ESTIMATING THE PROPORTION OF FACULTY WHO WOULD WORK PAST AGE 70

The committee examined the relatively sparse evidence on faculty who choose to work past age 70, as well as the more extensive evidence on the number of faculty now working past age 65. In this section we concentrate on evidence of faculty age distributions and retirement patterns in higher education as a whole; in the next section we examine variations in retirement patterns by institutional type.

### Faculty Near Retirement Age

Future retirement trends depend partly on present age distributions, that is, the number of faculty who will be old enough to consider retirement (e.g., age 60 or older) at any given time. Therefore, we first looked at the age distribution of faculty and how it has changed over the past decade.

Estimates of the age distribution from three national samples of faculty members are remarkably similar (see Figure 1). The longitudinal Survey of Doctorate Recipients (SDR), conducted every 2 years by the National Research Council, includes information on the ages of faculty members with doctorates. Data from cross-sectional surveys—the U.S. Department of Education's 1988 National Survey of Post-Secondary Faculty (NSOPF) and the 1989 survey of faculty conducted by the Higher Education Research Institute (HERI) at the University of California at Los Angeles—include faculty members with and without doctoral degrees (see Appendix B for details on the three surveys, including a discussion of methodological issues and suggestions for future survey research).

The committee was cautious in its use of these survey data. For example, in examining the SDR, we learned that the unweighted numbers of respondents in the 65+ and 70+ age categories are too low as a proportion of the estimated population to support detailed projections even from weighted data (see Appendix B). This limitation prevents us from calculating faculty

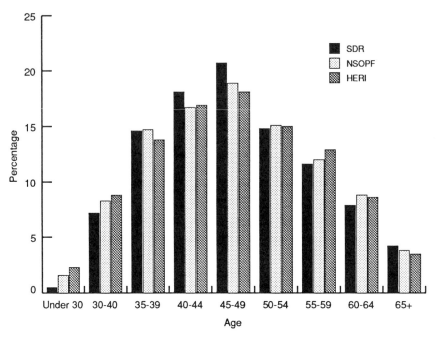

FIGURE 1    Faculty age profiles from three surveys. *Note:* Summary of Doctorate Recipients (SDR), National Survey of Postsecondary Faculty (NSOPF), Higher Education Research Institute (HERI).

retirement rates using SDR data; however, the consistency between the age distributions found by the three surveys allows us to draw some conclusions.

Although the three surveys used different sampling techniques and sample sizes, all three data sets show that less than 5 percent of the faculty members are age 65 or older. Less than one-half of 1 percent of the faculty in the SDR and NSOPF samples are over age 70. The data do not allow us to estimate the exact number of current, retired, and deceased faculty over age 65, but they do suggest that large numbers of faculty begin to retire around age 65 and that most retire before the current mandatory retirement age of 70.

Over the past decade, the age distribution of faculty with doctorates (see Table 1) shows an increase in the average age of faculty. The current age distribution suggests that an increasing proportion of faculty will be approaching retirement over the next two decades, with the largest age group of current faculty entering their 60s in a little more than 10 years. Table 1 shows that the percentage of faculty age 65 or older increased from 2.1 to 4.0 from 1979 to 1989; this percentage change represented about

TABLE 1    Faculty Age Profile, 1979-1989 (in percent)

| Age | 1979 | 1981 | 1983 | 1985 | 1987 | 1989 |
|-----|------|------|------|------|------|------|
| Under 30 | 1.6 | 1.2 | 0.7 | 0.7 | 0.6 | 0.5 |
| 30-34 | 12.9 | 11.3 | 8.7 | 8.3 | 7.0 | 7.2 |
| 35-39 | 22.5 | 19.5 | 17.3 | 16.0 | 14.8 | 14.6 |
| 40-44 | 18.0 | 20.3 | 22.2 | 21.3 | 19.5 | 18.2 |
| 45-49 | 14.7 | 14.8 | 16.3 | 17.7 | 20.7 | 20.8 |
| 50-54 | 12.1 | 12.9 | 13.4 | 13.6 | 14.8 | 14.8 |
| 55-59 | 10.1 | 10.5 | 10.9 | 10.8 | 11.0 | 11.6 |
| 60-64 | 6.0 | 6.7 | 8.0 | 8.0 | 8.0 | 7.9 |
| 65-69 | 2.0 | 2.6 | 2.6 | 3.1 | 3.2 | 3.5 |
| 70+ | 0.1 | 0.2 | 0.3 | 0.4 | 0.5 | 0.5 |

*Source:* Survey of Doctorate Recipients.

5,000 faculty members. Given the increase in the mandatory retirement age from 65 to 70 for the period from 1978 to 1982, the number of faculty aged 65 or older is still small. This suggests that most faculty members choose to retire before age 65.

## Faculty Likely to Work Past Age 70

In order to estimate the number of faculty who will work past age 70, one needs to know not only the number of retirement-age faculty but also how likely those faculty are to retire at earlier or later ages. The national faculty surveys provide some evidence on the number of faculty at given ages to continue working past age 70, but their data do not support calculations of the proportion of faculty at any given age who retire—that is, of retirement rates. Furthermore, most studies of faculty retirement concentrate on average retirement ages rather than the proportion of faculty retiring at higher than average ages. Studies of faculty retirement behavior do, however, cast light on the propensity of older faculty to continue working. Some faculty members who retired at age 70 might have worked longer had they been permitted to do so.

In contrast to recent national trends toward earlier retirements, college and university faculty median retirement ages have not decreased (Burkhauser and Quinn, 1989:66). However, the available data and research results suggest that few faculty have chosen to work until age 70 or older. One limitation to these data and research reports is that most faculty retirees are white males. If women or minority faculty have significantly different retirement patterns, future faculty retirement patterns will change to reflect this. Table 2 shows the age distribution of all U.S. faculty in higher education.

TABLE 2   Regular Full-Time Instructional Faculty in U.S. Institutions of Higher Education by Age, Gender, and Race or Ethnicity

| Faculty Characteristics | Number (in thousands) | Age (in percent) | | | | | | | |
|---|---|---|---|---|---|---|---|---|---|
| | | ≤29 | 30-34 | 35-39 | 40-44 | 45-49 | 50-54 | 55-59 | ≤60 |
| Male | 355 | 1.2 | 7.1 | 13.0 | 15.9 | 19.4 | 15.8 | 13.5 | 14.1 |
| Female | 133 | 2.7 | 11.4 | 19.1 | 18.9 | 17.6 | 13.3 | 8.2 | 8.7 |
| White, non-Hispanic | 437 | 1.5 | 8.0 | 14.3 | 16.5 | 18.8 | 15.2 | 12.4 | 13.2 |
| Asian | 21 | 3.2 | 14.8 | 17.5 | 15.5 | 18.5 | 14.2 | 9.1 | 7.5 |
| Black, non-Hispanic | 16 | 1.0 | 8.6 | 17.9 | 20.8 | 22.4 | 12.7 | 6.7 | 9.8 |
| Hispanic | 11 | 1.6 | 5.6 | 17.3 | 22.6 | 23.4 | 10.9 | 10.8 | 7.8 |
| American Indian | 4 | 0.0 | 9.2 | 21.9 | 11.4 | 6.8 | 30.2 | 15.4 | 5.1 |

*Note:* Data are for all public and private not-for-profit institutions that grant a 2-year or higher degree and whose accreditation at the higher education level is recognized by the U.S. Department of Education. Percentage distributions may not add to 100 because of rounding; number of faculty may not add to total because of rounding or missing data.

*Source:* Special tabulation, U.S. Department of Education, National Center for Education Statistics, National Survey of Postsecondary Faculty (NSOPF) 1988; data for fall 1987.

Furthermore, attitudes about an "appropriate" retirement age could change in the future, perhaps in response to some of the factors that affect retirement behavior (e.g., economic conditions, health care benefits, and state of health). Existing data show that retirement patterns do not change swiftly and may proceed at a generational pace (Burkhauser and Quinn, 1989). People who have worked for several decades with the expectation that they would retire around age 65 or 70 may be less likely to change their expectations than those just starting careers.

## Retirement Patterns at Uncapped Colleges and Universities

Some states and individual colleges and universities have already eliminated mandatory retirement for tenured faculty. Figure 2 shows the status of uncapped public and private institutions at the time of this report's publication. More than one-third of the states have eliminated mandatory retirement for tenured faculty in public colleges and universities, and some states have also eliminated mandatory retirement in private colleges and universities. In addition to institutions uncapped by state law, some public and private institutions have independently decided to uncap. Although most uncapped colleges and universities have eliminated mandatory retirement during the past 3 years, public higher education systems in three states—Florida, Maine, and Wisconsin—have been uncapped for long enough to

| All Colleges and Universities | Public Colleges and Universities |
|---|---|
| Hawaii | Alaska[a] |
| Maine | Alabama[b] |
| Montana | Arizona |
| Nevada | Connecticut |
| Utah | Florida |
| Wisconsin | Idaho |
| Puerto Rico | Louisiana[c] |
| | New Hampshire[d] |
| | New York |
| | Texas |
| | Virginia |
| | Wyoming[e] |

[a]Alaska Pacific University is the state's only private institution with a tenure system; it has voluntarily eliminated mandatory retirement.

[b]The following 4-year public institutions have no mandatory retirement age: Alabama State University; Auburn University, Main Campus and Montgomery; Livingston University; Troy State University, Main Campus and Montgomery; University of Montevalla; and University of South Alabama (Source: Wilner, 1990).

[c]State law specifically exempts police officers and fire fighters but not faculty.

[d]Except for vocational and technical schools.

[e]There are no private colleges or universities in Wyoming.

FIGURE 2    States that have eliminated mandatory retirement.

provide more than 1 or 2 years' data on changing faculty retirement behavior. In two of those states—Maine and Wisconsin—state law also uncapped private colleges and universities, most of which are liberal arts colleges.

Given the limited national survey data on the number of faculty over age 70, the experiences of uncapped colleges and universities provide the only available direct information on faculty retirement ages in the absence of a mandatory retirement age. The committee requested data on faculty ages and retirement ages from state higher education systems and state retirement systems in uncapped states, and it conducted case studies at public and private uncapped institutions. In all, we found few faculty chose to continue working past age 70, although faculty retirement choices at many colleges and universities may have been affected by the introduction of retirement incentive programs as well as by uncapping.

• In Florida the average retirement age for all university employees (the state retirement system cannot separate data on faculty) has remained remarkably stable at around age 63 since the state eliminated mandatory retirement in 1976. Data on the average retirement age of tenured faculty at one institution, the University of Florida at Gainesville, show that annual average retirement ages from 1972 to 1989 varied from 61 to 64, with no upward trend over the period. The university reports that 1.6 percent of the faculty are aged 70 or older.

• The University of Maine system benefits coordinator reported that the average faculty retirement age has been between 61 and 63 both prior to uncapping in 1978 and subsequently. Only 6 of the 1,370 faculty (0.4 percent) are over age 70.

• The University of Wisconsin could not provide longitudinal data, but data from the Madison campus on the ages of the 97 faculty members who have retired since February 1989 show that the average faculty retirement age was 65 and that 14 of the retirees (14 percent) were aged 70 or over. Of the 2,368 faculty members, 26 (1.1 percent) are over age 70.

On the basis of their study of the retirement patterns of tenured arts and science faculty at 19 public and private universities and 14 private liberal arts colleges, Rees and Smith (1991) identified several factors that may explain differences in mean retirement ages among institutions. The presence of a mandatory retirement age was not one of them. In fact, for their sample of uncapped liberal arts colleges, the mean retirement age of tenured faculty is 1 year lower than the mean retirement age at capped institutions. Rees and Smith also found that the mean retirement age at uncapped colleges did not change after the end of mandatory retirement. Of course, a constant mean retirement age at an uncapped college could mask later retirement of some faculty offset by earlier retirements of other faculty.

The few colleges and universities that have been uncapped for a long enough period that faculty could have continued working until their late 70s or early 80s report that few individuals have taken advantage of this opportunity. The committee's case studies of uncapped colleges and universities found that only one or two faculty in uncapped institutions have stayed past age 73. The oldest two retirees in the University of Wisconsin-Madison data were 74, and, as noted above, only 1.1 percent of the faculty are over age 70. The proportion of faculty over age 70 is small (no more than 1.6 percent), even at colleges and universities that have been uncapped for over a decade. We note that none of these uncapped institutions is a private research university. Johns Hopkins University, the only private research university uncapped at the time of our study, stopped enforcing mandatory retirement when the ADEA amendments passed in 1986 and formally uncapped in 1989. Of their 1,974 faculty, 4 (0.2 percent) are over age 70.

### Effects of Raising the Age Cap from 65 to 70

In 1978 Congress required colleges and universities to raise the mandatory retirement age for tenured faculty from 65 to 70 by July 1, 1982.

Changes in retirement patterns over this period can provide some insight into the proportion of faculty choosing to postpone retirement when they have the opportunity to do so, but one cannot simply compare average faculty retirement ages before and after 1982. Although the 1978 ADEA amendments set a deadline for raising the mandatory retirement age, a 1980 study of 278 institutions found that prior to the 1978 amendments, one-third of all institutions already had no mandatory retirement age or a mandatory retirement age higher than 65. Several states raised or abolished the mandatory retirement age prior to the 1982 deadline. Furthermore, institutional retirement policies were apparently flexible: At colleges and universities with a stated mandatory retirement age of 65, 40 percent of the faculty members reaching age 65 continued to work (Holden and Hansen, 1989:38).

In their study of faculty retirement ages at 101 colleges and universities, Lozier and Dooris (1990:14) found that the overall average retirement age at all institutions was less than 65: It was age 63.8 at institutions that raised the cap in 1982 and age 64.3 at institutions with a mandatory retirement age of 70 during the entire study period of 1981-1988. Another study of retirement patterns at 36 colleges and universities (mostly private) found that the average faculty retirement age increased by slightly less than 1.5 years, from age 64.6 to age 66.0, from 1982 to 1986 (Consortium on Financing Higher Education, 1987).

## Conclusions

Nationwide, faculty retirement patterns have remained fairly stable for the last 15 years despite a major change in retirement law between 1977 and 1982. At the uncapped institutions for which there are data on faculty ages, the proportion of faculty over age 70 was less than 1.6 percent. The observed faculty retirement behavior may be influenced by factors other than uncapping. For example, many of these institutions offer retirement incentive programs. Data from case studies of institutions uncapped for more than 3 years show that of the few faculty who have chosen to work past age 70, almost all retired by age 73.

On the basis of our consideration of the available data and studies, we conclude: **Most faculty do not choose to work until age 70, although they have the opportunity to do so, and, overall, only a small number of the nation's tenured faculty will continue working in their current positions past age 70.**

## VARIATION IN FACULTY RETIREMENT PATTERNS

National averages and the experiences of individual colleges and universities cannot describe or predict variations in faculty retirement behavior across more than 3,200 institutions of higher education or by fields. Therefore, in this section we examine evidence on whether faculty retirement patterns differ by types of institution. In order to make our examination of institutional variation more manageable, the committee used a set of broad institutional classifications constructed by the Carnegie Foundation for the Advancement of Teaching. These classifications divide colleges and universities based on whether they are public or private, on enrollment, on research spending, on number and types of degrees awarded, and on range of subjects offered. There are six broad categories (see Appendix C for details):

• *research universities*—about 100 public and private universities that offer the widest range and level of degrees, including at least 50 Ph.D.s annually, and with at least $12.5 million in annual research support;

• *doctorate-granting universities*—more than 100 universities that offer a wide range of subjects and degrees, including 20 or more Ph.D.s annually in one discipline or 10 or more Ph.D.s annually in three or more disciplines;

• *comprehensive colleges and universities*—about 600 public and private institutions that offer a wide range of degrees up to the master's level (some also award a few doctorates) and that enroll at least 1,500 students;

• *liberal arts colleges*—more than 550 colleges that award mostly bachelor's degrees;

• *2-year colleges*—nearly 1,400 colleges, three-quarters of which are public, that offer Associate of Arts degrees and adult training in a wide range of fields; and

• *specialized institutions*—more than 600 institutions that offer degrees in one or two specialties, such as the traditional professions (e.g., law, medicine) and fine arts.

The number of faculty in any institution or field who would work past age 70 if allowed to do so can be discussed in terms of the number of faculty reaching age 70 and the proportion who would choose to keep working. The age distribution of faculty by selected subgroups reveals that some institutions and fields face a more immediate increase in the number of faculty nearing traditional retirement ages (60-70 years). Others face an increase several years in the future, and still others are likely to have a consistent number of faculty reaching retirement age over time. Figures 3 and 4 depict the variations in the age distribution of faculty with doctorates by type of institution and by selected field of study, based on the 1989 SDR data.

In comparison with other institutional categories, comprehensive colleges and universities have a higher proportion of faculty aged 45-55 so that a greater proportion of their faculty members will reach retirement age (60 or older) in 10-20 years. Liberal arts colleges and doctoral universities appear to follow the overall age distribution for higher education. Research

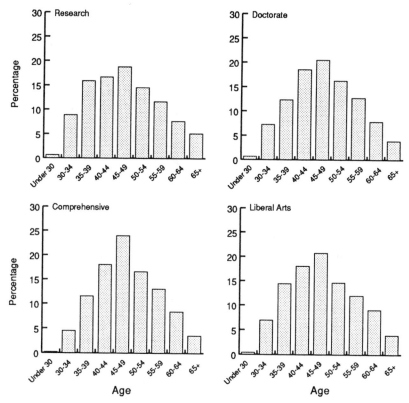

FIGURE 3  Faculty age profiles by type of institution.

universities have a higher percentage of faculty in the youngest age groups (under age 40) and the oldest age group (over 65 years) and a correspondingly lower percentage of faculty members in the middle years.

Fewer data are available on the age distribution of faculty at 2-year colleges: The SDR is not an appropriate source because approximately 75 percent of community college faculty do not have doctorates so other sources must be sought. The Commission on the Future of Community Colleges (1988:5) of the American Association of the Community and Junior Colleges reported that total enrollment in 2-year colleges grew by 240 between 1965 and 1975, and James Palmer (Center for Community College Education, George Mason University) reported (private communication) that a high proportion of the current faculty were hired at that time. The commission (1988:12) also found that "the average full-time community college faculty member is 50 years of age," and it estimated that approximately 40 percent of all community college faculty would retire by the year 2000.

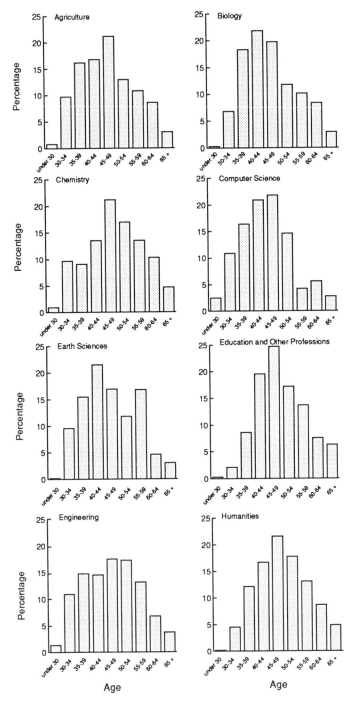

FIGURE 4   Faculty age profiles by field.

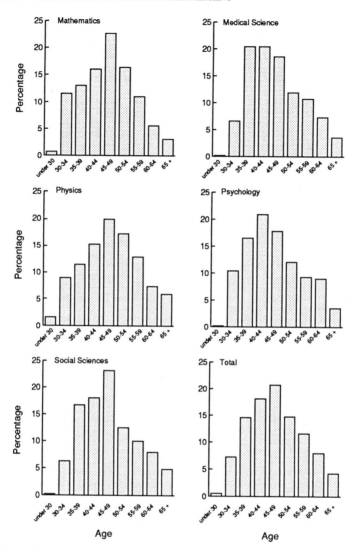

FIGURE 4  *Continued*

These sources, as well as our case studies of individual community colleges, suggest that few community college faculty retire later than age 65 and almost no one retires after age 70.

Faculty age profiles also vary by field. For example, faculty in computer science are younger on average than faculty in other disciplines. Only a relatively small proportion of computer science and medical faculty members with doctorates will be approaching retirement over the next 15 years. In contrast, chemistry has a smaller-than-average percentage of faculty aged

35-45 and a comparatively larger proportion of faculty approaching retirement age during the next two decades. In the humanities relatively large proportions of the faculty are in the middle and older age groups.

Variations in the age distribution of faculty by type of institution and by field do not indicate what proportion of these faculty will retire at any specific age; rather, retirement rates need to be estimated in order to project the numbers of faculty who would work past age 70. The numbers of older faculty in the national data bases and from other studies are too small to divide further into subgroups. Therefore, some researchers have applied retirement rates from statistics on all faculty to the age distributions of faculty in individual fields and types of institutions.

With a constant retirement rate, the numbers of retirements depend on the number of retirement-age faculty. For example, Bowen and Sosa (1989:198) apply retirement rates drawn from a 1987 Lozier and Dooris survey of 20 universities to data from the 1977 and 1987 SDRs to project future retirements for arts and sciences faculty. They project that greater proportions of faculty at comprehensive institutions and research universities—the two types of institutions with higher numbers of faculty in the middle and older age groups—will retire in the next 10 years.

In the most recent study of this type, Lozier and Dooris (1990) used data on faculty retiring from 101 4-year colleges and universities to project that, by the academic year 2002-2003, the number of faculty retiring annually will be 25-40 percent higher than in 1987-1988. By field, they project that the number of humanities faculty who retire will peak during the period from 1988 to 1993, the number of life sciences faculty who retire will increase through the mid 1990s and then return to current levels, the number of mathematics and physical sciences faculty who retire will increase modestly but steadily throughout the period, and the number of behavioral and social sciences faculty who retire will decline during the mid to late 1990s and then return to current levels (Lozier and Dooris, 1990:58). Using Lozier and Dooris's earlier (1988) higher estimates of faculty retirement rates, Bowen and Sosa (1989) projected similar variations in numbers of retirements by field.

The number of faculty who retire (or do not retire) in a given discipline or type of institution depends not only on the number of faculty old enough to retire but also on the propensity of faculty in that discipline or type of institution to postpone retirement past age 70. These rates may not be constant, as assumed above, but the numbers of older faculty in available studies are too small to support calculations of retirement rates by fields. (The medical school faculty register of the Association of American Medical Colleges was large enough, but it was not structured to support analyses of changing faculty age distributions or retirement patterns.) The data we were able to collect from individual colleges and universities show variations in faculty retirement ages among different disciplines, but no one discipline or set of disciplines had consistently different retirement ages.

There is, however, evidence that faculty at some types of institutions are more likely to postpone retirement. Lozier and Dooris (1990) used data from a survey of more than 500 retired faculty from 101 colleges and universities, divided into liberal arts, comprehensive, and a category combining doctoral and research universities. They found an average retirement age of 64.3 for faculty at doctoral and research universities, 63.5 for liberal arts colleges, and 63.6 for comprehensive institutions (1990:17). However, combining research and doctoral universities could mask differences between those categories. A survey of faculty by the Carnegie Foundation (Carnegie Foundation for the Advancement of Teaching, 1989:87) found that faculty at research universities were least likely to report looking forward to retirement: 69 percent in comparison to 75 percent for all faculty.

Evidence on retirement patterns at individual colleges and universities also suggests that faculty at research universities retire, on average, at later ages. Rees and Smith (1991:21-22) found that the mean age at retirement was 1.45 years higher for research university faculty than for faculty at the other universities and liberal arts colleges in their sample of 33 colleges and universities. In all, 35.1 percent of the faculty who retired from capped private universities (including three universities not classified as research) did so at the mandatory age. At capped public universities, 17.8 percent of the faculty retired at age 70 or later; at uncapped public universities, 25.1 percent of the faculty did so. In comparison, few faculty at the liberal arts colleges in the Rees and Smith sample (all private) retired at or above age 70: 4.3 percent at uncapped colleges and 11.5 percent at capped colleges. The Consortium on Financing Higher Education (COFHE) (1987:13) found that, at the 36 colleges and universities it surveyed, the percentage of faculty members retiring at age 70 between 1982 and 1986 varied from 0 to 83 percent. At 7 of the 21 universities that provided data to COFHE—Harvard, Princeton, Stanford, the University of Chicago, the University of Pennsylvania, the University of Toronto, and Yale—more than 40 percent of the faculty who retired did so at age 70. In comparison, only one of the seven liberal arts colleges in the COFHE sample—Williams College—had more than 40 percent of its retirees stay to the mandatory age.

The percentage of faculty who retire at age 70 may be more significant for projecting the number of faculty who will postpone retirement than data on average retirement ages. Lozier and Dooris (1990:44-47) report that 80 percent of the retirees in their study said that the mandatory retirement age was not important in their retirement decision. However, 87 percent of the faculty who retired at age 70 said that, without mandatory retirement, they would have continued working, on average, to age 74.5.

Retirement age differences between institutions may be explained by differences in mission and student quality. Rees and Smith (1991) used regression analyses to predict the age of faculty retiring at or above age 70 for their sample of colleges and universities. They found quality of the student body (measured by average Scholastic Aptitude Test [SAT] scores) is the strongest predictor of delayed retirement, followed by low teaching loads and holding research grants. Rees and Smith suggest that faculty are more willing to continue working when they have good students, low teaching loads, and a funded research agenda.

Faculty tend to retire later at private colleges and universities than at public colleges and universities. Lozier and Dooris (1990:17) found that the average retirement age for faculty from private institutions was 65.3, compared to 63.5 with faculty from public institutions. COFHE (1987) found that 31 percent of the faculty who retired from private institutions did so at the mandatory age, compared with 20 percent for faculty from public institutions. However, some of these differences may be due to variations in teaching loads, student quality, and levels of faculty retirement income rather than to whether the institution is public or private. Rees and Smith discovered no differences in retirement patterns between the public and private research institutions in their more homogenous sample.

The committee requested data on the age of faculty who retired at age 70 or older from universities with the highest reported research and development expenditure, divided where possible by schools within the universities. Some other colleges and universities also provided us with these data. These data, like those from the 1987 COFHE study, show that there is considerable variance in retirement behavior within as well as among institutional types (see Table 3). Most of the few uncapped universities were not able to provide data on their faculty retirement patterns. Ten institutions—the University of California system, the University of Chicago, Columbia University, Duke University, Harvard University, Massachusetts Institute of Technology, the University of Pennsylvania, Princeton University, Stanford University, and Yale University—reported that more than one-third of their faculty who retired did so at age 70 or older. The University of California at Irvine, the University of Chicago (except its medical school), Columbia's Arts and Sciences Division, Harvard, and Yale reported that more than one-half of their faculty who retired did so at age 70 or older (see Table 3). The faculty retirement data thus suggest that at some research universities high proportions of faculty will choose to work past age 70, but the data do not suggest any way to distinguish which universities they will be. Some of the variation in faculty retirement patterns may be due to different retirement incentive programs offered by some institutions.

TABLE 3 Faculty Who Retired at Age 70 or Older at Selected Universities

| University | Years Covered | Faculty Who Retired | | | COFHE 1982-1986 Percent |
|---|---|---|---|---|---|
| | | ≥70 | All | Percent | |
| California Institute of Technology | 1985-1990 | 9 | 29 | 31 | — |
| California, University of | 1985-1988 | 149 | 429 | 35 | — |
| Berkeley | | 47 | 108 | 44 | — |
| Davis | | 16 | 84 | 19 | — |
| Irvine | | 10 | 18 | 56 | — |
| Los Angeles | | 43 | 97 | 44 | — |
| Riverside | | 5 | 25 | 20 | — |
| San Diego | | 12 | 25 | 48 | — |
| San Francisco | | 8 | 22 | 36 | — |
| Santa Barbara | | 8 | 39 | 20 | — |
| Santa Cruz | | 0 | 11 | 0 | — |
| Chicago | 1985-1990 | 55 | 86 | 64 | — |
| Chicago Medical | 1985-1990 | 11 | 28 | 39 | — |
| Columbia | | | | | 25 |
| Columbia Arts and Sciences | 1985-1990 | 28 | 52 | 53 | — |
| Columbia Medical | 1985-1989 | 0 | 17 | 0 | — |
| Cornell | 1986-1990 | 40 | 162 | 25 | 38 |
| Duke | 1985-1990 | 37 | 95 | 39 | 38 |
| George Washington | 1989-1990 | 3 | 13 | 19 | — |
| Harvard Arts and Sciences | 1986-1990 | 23 | 30 | 77 | 45 |
| Harvard Medical | 1986-1990 | 34 | 40 | 85 | — |
| Illinois, University of | 1985-1990 | 68 | 537 | 13 | 10 |
| Massachusetts Institute of Technology | 1986-1990 | 21 | 59 | 36 | 10 |
| Miami, University of | 1986-1990 | 14 | 49 | 28 | — |
| Michigan, University of | 1985-1990 | 46 | 284 | 16 | 31 |
| Michigan State | 1986-1990 | 45 | 302 | 15 | 31 |
| Pennsylvania State | 1987-1989 | 1 | 18 | 6 | — |
| Pennsylvania, University of | 1984-1988 | 46 | 120 | 38 | 66 |
| School of Medicine | 1984-1988 | 20 | 41 | 49 | — |
| Princeton | 1985-1990 | 21 | 54 | 39 | 56 |
| Stanford Humanities and Sciences | 1985-1989 | 16 | 42 | 38 | 59 |
| Texas A&M | 1985-1989 | 7 | 77 | 9 | — |
| Yale (excluding medical)[a] | 1985-1990 | 42 | 55 | 76 | 83 |

*Note:* These universities had a mandatory retirement age of 70 for the years covered by the committee's data.

[a]Phased retirement program participants counted as employed.

On the basis of these data, the committee concludes: **At some research universities a high proportion of faculty would choose to remain employed past age 70 if allowed to do so.** Faculty at research universities are more likely than faculty elsewhere to have low teaching loads, relatively high-quality undergraduates, and the facilities to support research grants—the factors Rees and Smith found best predicted delayed retirements.

## ESTIMATING THE EFFECTS OF UNCAPPING AT THREE UNIVERSITIES

Any college or university at which a significant proportion of faculty decide to continue working past age 70 will experience faculty hiring reductions, cost increases, or both. In this section we estimate the magnitude of possible effects on faculty hiring and institutional budgets at universities at which faculty are most likely to work past 70. We also consider whether reduced hiring will limit opportunities for new faculty members. (We examine the consequences for faculty and institutional quality of reduced faculty hiring in Chapter 3, and we address ways to increase hiring by encouraging faculty retirements in Chapters 4 and 5.)

In order to project the effects of eliminating mandatory retirement on faculty hiring and the budget at a given institution, one must consider the current age distribution of its faculty members and the rate at which faculty of different ages enter and leave the institution. For example, some institutions do most of their hiring at the assistant professor level, and other institutions hire more midcareer faculty members. Likewise, faculty leave institutions at different ages and for different reasons: denial of tenure, acceptance of a position elsewhere, poor health, death, or retirement.

Administrators at a few colleges and universities use "faculty flow models" to estimate the numbers of faculty entering and leaving their institutions, as well as the age distribution of their faculty and the size of their budget (see, e.g., Hopkins and Massy, 1981). The modeler must specify the rate at which faculty enter or leave for each period, using historic data on hiring, resignations, retirements, and deaths. Based on the age distribution and the entering and leaving rates of faculty in each age category, the models then project faculty hiring and age distributions for successive time periods. Such models can also project future salary costs on the basis of estimates of the average salary of faculty in each age group. These models allow colleges and universities to examine the effects of policy changes on the composition and costs of their faculty.

The committee projected potential effects of uncapping on hiring, using data provided by three research universities that have a mandatory retirement age of 70 and at which a significant proportion of faculty may postpone retirement past age 70 if mandatory retirement is eliminated. Two of these institutions examined some of the potential effects using their own faculty flow models and data on their arts and science faculty. For the third institution, the committee used a model it adapted from one designed by Biedenweg and Keenan (1989) to examine data supplied by the university. At university A a committee of faculty and administrators found that 64 percent of the faculty aged 60-64 remained employed after age 65. At university B a committee of faculty and administrators reported that 60 percent of tenured faculty in arts and science who retired did so at age 70. At university C more than 50 percent of the arts and science faculty who retire do so at the mandatory age.

The university A and B committees took different approaches to estimating the age of older faculty likely to retire after age 70. As a low estimate of changed behavior after uncapping (i.e., most faculty continue to retire before age 70), the university A committee assumed that the proportion of faculty who remain employed past age 65 would not change and that 25 percent of the faculty who worked past age 65 would continue to work past age 70. As a high estimate (i.e., more faculty retire after age 70), the university A committee assumed that the percentage of faculty who remained employed beyond age 65 would increase from 64 percent to 75 percent, and 50 percent of the faculty who worked after age 65 would also work after age 70.

In order to test the sensitivity of these assumptions, we ran our model using estimates of faculty working past age 70 that were both higher and lower than those provided by university A. The results show the model to be relatively insensitive to retirement or retention rates, because the total number of faculty reaching age 70 at university A is relatively low during the next 15 years.

The university B committee made projections using estimates of the percentage of faculty over age 70 who would continue to work each year after uncapping: 75 percent (low) and 90 percent (high). In other words, for the low estimate 25 percent of the faculty over age 70 retire each year, and for the high estimate 10 percent retire each year. In comparison to university A, university B assumed no increase in the proportion of faculty reaching age 70. Our committee also applied the university B assumptions (75 percent and 90 percent) to University C's model and faculty data.

The magnitude of cost increases or the limit on future hiring resulting from decreased turnover depend heavily on an institution's policy choices. We examined the potential impact of uncapping on hiring and budgets with three separate options: constant faculty size, constant budget, and constant hiring. A college or university can choose to maintain the current size of its faculty by hiring faculty at a slower rate. It can also maintain a constant salary budget, which, since salaries rise with age, will limit hiring still further. (Data on average salary by 5-year age group from universities A,

B, and C and from case study institutions show older faculty earn more on average, but there is little increase between ages 61-65 and 66-70. We have therefore assumed that faculty in the model who stay past age 70 will earn salaries equal to the average for faculty aged 66-70.) An institution could continue to hire new faculty at a steady rate regardless of postponed retirements, which maintains hiring flexibility but increases costs. Lastly, it could choose a policy other than constant budget, salary, or hiring, such as hiring a few more faculty members than it needs to fill openings but hiring fewer faculty annually than it has hired in past years. Table 4 summarizes the projected effects on each institution in terms of its increased salary costs or decreased hiring in comparison with its salary costs and hiring projected if no faculty member works past age 70 and faculty size is constant. This comparison presents the projected decrease in hiring due to uncapping, but it underestimates the total reductions in hiring expected at university C, which had planned to decrease its faculty size.

TABLE 4   Effects of Uncapping Projected by Faculty Flow Models for Three Universities (A, B, C)

a. Decrease in Number of Faculty Hired (in percent)

| Time | Assumption: Constant Faculty Size | | | Assumption: Constant Faculty Salary Budget | | |
|------|------|------|------|------|------|------|
| | A | B | C | A | B[a] | C |
| First 5 years | 5-14 | 19-31 | 5-8 | 9-21 | - | 7-12 |
| After 15 years | 2-4 | 4-10 | 3-7 | 1-3 | - | 2-9 |

b. Increase in Salary Budget in Real Dollars (in percent)

| Time | Assumption: Constant Faculty Size | | | Assumption: Constant Faculty Hiring Rate | | |
|------|------|------|------|------|------|------|
| | A | B[a] | C | A | B[a] | C |
| First 5 years | 1-2 | - | 1-2 | 2-4 | - | 4-5 |
| After 15 years | 1-2 | - | 1-2 | 1-1 | - | 4-8 |

*Note:* Low estimates for A: 64 percent retire after age 65; 25 percent of these retire after age 70. High estimates for A: 75 percent retire after age 65; 50 percent of these retire after age 70. Low estimates for B and C: 75 percent of faculty over age 70 continue working each year. High estimates for B and C: 90 percent of faculty over age 70 continue working each year.

[a]University B did not calculate cost effects.

## Constant Faculty Size

Several letter survey respondents stated that postponed faculty retirements would create a decrease in hiring because an increase in faculty career length means a decrease in faculty turnover. One letter survey respondent assumed colleges and universities would attempt to maintain a constant faculty size and pointed out the cost of this policy:

> Given a fixed faculty size, if some faculty members stay on beyond age 70 . . . elimination of a mandatory retirement age will inevitably reduce the ability of the institution to hire young faculty . . . and also limit our ability to respond to unexpected developments that would call for new faculty members in certain fields.

The assumption of a fixed number of faculty positions is most applicable to public colleges and universities in states in which the number of faculty is set by the legislature. We estimated the extent to which hiring would be reduced if the three universities for which we have data held faculty size constant after uncapping. Projected hiring reductions in the first 5-year period after uncapping range from 5 percent at university A using its low estimate to 31 percent at university B using its high estimate (see Table 4a).

The projected number of positions that become available eventually rises at all three universities as faculty who postponed retirement begin to retire, but the projected number of positions remains below the levels expected with mandatory retirement. After 15 years the projected decrease in hiring ranges from 2 percent to 15 percent less than levels projected if all faculty retire by age 70. In the interim period, however, patterns vary. At university A after 5 years, the projected number of positions falls even further and then begins to rise after about 10 years. University B expects fewer open positions for the 5-15 years after uncapping, regardless of mandatory retirement policy, because of a decrease in the proportion of current faculty who will reach retirement age. Using university B's low estimate, university C shows 5 percent fewer positions in the first 5 years and 8 percent fewer positions in both periods using the higher estimate. These results are within the range projected by Southworth and Jagmin (1979), who modeled faculty flows for the colleges and universities belonging to the Consortium on Financing Higher Education as a way to estimate the effects of raising the mandatory retirement age from 65 to 70.

A constant faculty size does not imply a constant faculty budget. Salaries tend to increase with age; thus, an increase in the average age of an institution's faculty increases overall costs. For university A, projected real salary costs increase overall by 2 percent over the first 5 years using the high estimate of postponed retirements and 1 percent using the low estimate. For university C, projected costs increase by about 2 percent over the first 5 years after uncapping using the high estimate. (University B did not calculate cost effects.)

## Constant Budget

Few colleges and universities in the United States would find it easy to cover the cost increases associated with a larger faculty size. A college or university that is facing higher costs because of postponed faculty retirements might look to decreases in hiring as one mechanism to balance its budget. Using this assumption in the models yields a "worst case scenario" in the sense that all expense cuts come from the academic salary budget.

For university A's high estimate, the constant budget model projects 21 percent fewer faculty hired in the first 5 years after uncapping, in comparison with 14 percent fewer in the constant faculty size model. Total faculty size decreases by 2 percent. The model projects that some of the lost positions could be reinstated 15 years after uncapping, but as in the constant faculty size model, the rate of faculty turnover remains lower than that projected with mandatory retirement. With a constant budget the projected size of the faculty also levels off at a new, lower level. For university A's low estimates, the number of faculty hired and the size of the faculty initially decrease by 9 percent and 1 percent, respectively. They then rise gradually through successive 5-year periods, matching the levels expected with mandatory retirement 20 years after uncapping.

When costs are held constant in university C's model, using university B's high estimate, projected hiring is 12 percent less than if all faculty retire by age 70, in comparison with the 8 percent less projected using the constant faculty size assumption.

## Constant Hiring

When we incorporated the average salary for faculty in each age range in the constant faculty size models, we found that uncapping causes projected faculty salary budgets to increase from 1 to 3 percent, depending on the estimated proportion of faculty who postpone retirement past age 70. Continuing to hire new faculty in an attempt to cover new fields would be even more costly. If an institution continued to hire new faculty at a rate greater than the rate at which faculty were leaving, its faculty size would increase, and its costs would rise accordingly.

To estimate the magnitude of such an increase, we ran the model for university A holding the number of faculty hired in each time period equal to the number projected to be hired for the first 5-year time period with mandatory retirement. Projected real salary costs for the first to fifth year after uncapping are 2-4 percent higher than costs projected for the same period if all faculty retire by 70 (using the low or high projection of the proportion of faculty staying past age 70). The projected faculty size is 1-3 percent larger. When university C holds faculty hiring constant in its model, the projected costs in constant dollars of total faculty salary increase by 4-5 percent of the total salary budget in the first 5 years after uncapping. The university estimates that if it relied on tuition increases to pay for constant hiring, it would have to increase tuition by 3 percent just to cover the additional salary costs. If it relied on fundraising to cover the increase for the arts and sciences faculty salaries alone, it would need to raise a $30 million endowment. Furthermore, as the number of faculty increased, the institution would also have to pay for additional office space, laboratories, and support services.

As these figures suggest, an institution not planning to expand its faculty size has little opportunity to continue to hire if faculty postpone retirement. According to the provost at one research university, continued hiring is too expensive a strategy to use over an extended period:

> The effect of increasing the retirement age from age 65 to age 70 became significant as more and more faculty members chose to continue to the limit. Partly in response to the small number of retirements and partly in response to our perception that in some areas we would have a very large number of retirements occurring during a 2- or 3-year period in the early 1990s, we instituted an aggressive program of prefilling positions [i.e., hiring "replacements" in advance of an expected retirement]. While this strategy mitigated some of the effects of delayed retirements, it is quite clear that we have still offered fewer positions to young faculty members than would otherwise have been the case. If a substantial number of faculty members stay on beyond age 70, the effect will continue and become worse because we have committed all of the resources that could be made available to the present program and will not be able to continue with prefills as we have in the past.

At universities that are expanding, however, uncapping is unlikely to have major adverse affects. For example, in response to predictions that 63,000 additional students—over one-third of current student enrollment—will enroll by 2005, University of California system officials report plans to create three new campuses and increase enrollment and faculty size at seven of its nine campuses. Although these plans may be delayed because of state budget cuts, the system as a whole and all but two of its campuses, may eventually hire faculty at or in excess of former rates regardless of whether faculty members continue to work past age 70.

## Analysis of Projected Effects

These models estimate the consequences of different policy choices in isolation. Colleges and universities can respond to faculty members' remaining employed beyond age 70 by limiting any combination of hiring and faculty costs. A university might also cover additional faculty salary costs by limiting its expenditures for other categories of the budget, such as reducing support services or new construction, although any such reductions could have costs for the faculty and the institution. Colleges and universities could attempt to limit the number of postponed retirements by instituting programs designed to make retirement more attractive. However, financial incentives to retire or the provision of office space, support services, or other benefits for retirees create additional costs (see Chapters 4 and 5).

From a historical perspective, the projected effects of eliminating mandatory retirement on faculty hiring and on salary budgets are not extraordinary. The high inflation and energy costs of the 1970s caused greater financial hardship and more severe hiring constraints than are likely to result from changing mandatory retirement policy. The average age of faculty has risen and will continue to rise more because of the aging of current faculty than uncapping. The average age of faculty in the United States has been increasing because job growth in higher education leveled off during the 1970s and because of the possibly related increase in the average age of new Ph.D. recipients (Bowen, Lord, and Sosa, 1991).

Nevertheless, the committee recognizes that colleges and universities face severely limited sources of additional revenue. Most are already engaged in extensive fundraising. Research universities, including the universities most likely to be affected by the elimination of mandatory retirement, already struggle to balance their budgets, often through tuition increases that are well above the inflation rate. Additional salary costs or the cost of a retirement incentive program would add to existing fiscal pressures: State and federal funding of financial aid has been decreasing; federal support for overhead costs on grants is being reduced; new tax laws have limited fundraising; tax-exempt borrowing has been curtailed; other new tax regulations have forced institutions to cease offering unequal benefits to staff and faculty; new accounting regulations make retirement health benefits much more costly for private institutions; and colleges and universities face pressure to limit tuition increases. Few institutions expect the 1990s to match the 1980s in terms of economic growth, endowment growth, or low rates of inflation. The combination of these changes will make it more difficult for the universities most likely to be affected to adapt to the effects of uncapping. Thus, the elimination of mandatory retirement will have adverse effects on the budgets and hiring opportunities of some research universities.

For most faculty members the effects of eliminating mandatory retirement would be positive: They gain the right to choose a retirement age without any upper age limit on the choice. For some this future benefit may be partly offset by limited job opportunities in the present: Research universities adversely affected by uncapping will be forced to reduce their hiring or to undertake extraordinary fundraising activities to increase the number of available for positions, which suggests that they will have fewer positions available for either prospective new junior faculty or more senior faculty from other institutions. Since reduced rates of hiring will be confined to only some research universities, however, reductions in hiring are more likely to limit *where* faculty seeking research positions find jobs than *whether* they find jobs. Faculty who are qualified for positions at adversely affected research universities would be likely to attract offers from other research universities.

The committee's evidence shows the largest proportion of faculty are now aged 45-49, with the next largest group aged 40-44. Most of these faculty will not be considering retirement for at least 10-15 years. The effect of this "age bulge" on retirements will not take place until the end of this century or the beginning of the next.

Once those faculty in the bulge reach traditional retirement ages (i.e., age 60+), available evidence and projections indicate that the number of faculty retirements will increase, regardless of mandatory retirement. The committee, Lozier and Dooris (1990), and Bowen and Sosa (1989) all found that the likelihood of increased faculty retirements about 10 years from now is relatively insensitive to a range of possible future retirement rates. Colleges and universities will have increased faculty turnover. Cases of faculty continuing to work despite age-related declines in performance, although rare, could also increase. However, the lower numbers of faculty over age 50 suggest retirement levels will be relatively low in the coming decade. A decrease in the rate of retirements owing to uncapping at colleges and universities where the largest proportion of faculty are not yet near retirement could exacerbate expected low hiring levels.

A number of studies have projected a national shortage of faculty by combining information about the overall faculty age structure with estimates of future student enrollments, student/faculty ratios, and rates of departure from academia (Atkinson, 1990; Bowen and Schuster, 1986; Bowen and Sosa, 1989; El-Khawas, 1990). Some administrators and faculty have suggested that encouraging faculty to work past age 70 could alleviate impending shortages. Others have suggested that the effects of eliminating mandatory retirement are too small to affect faculty shortages. Still others have expressed a preference for the ability to hire now, rather than in the future when some researchers have projected that the numbers of prospective new faculty members will be lower and overall demand will be higher.

Because of variations in age distributions at individual colleges and universities, disciplines, and geographic regions, the most appropriate focus for analysis and policy making in response to these concerns is at those levels. Some colleges and universities—for example, those drawing on a regional base for students in areas with declining college-age population—may need fewer faculty in the future and not plan to replace all retiring faculty. Others, such as the University of California system, have proposed hiring a substantial number of additional faculty at certain campuses in response to projected enrollment increases.

## Conclusions

Despite the growing number of older faculty members in U.S. institutions of higher education, evidence from uncapped colleges and universities suggests that few tenured faculty now continue to work past 70. Current faculty retirement patterns suggest most faculty choose to retire before the mandatory retirement age. The committee concludes: **Higher education as a whole is likely to experience few changes in faculty behavior or demographics as a result of the elimination of mandatory retirement, and a significant number and proportion of faculty will choose to work past age 70 at a few research universities.**

Faculty at some research universities are more likely than faculty elsewhere to have low teaching loads, high-quality undergraduate and graduate students, and research support. Our analysis of the demographic and financial consequences of postponed faculty retirements leads us to believe that the ability of research universities to hire new faculty or control salary costs could be significantly lessened for a transition period of 5 to 15 years. Under certain circumstances there could be less severe long-term effects.

The effects of uncapping will not be the same at all colleges and universities or on all faculty. At some institutions more than one-quarter of the current tenured faculty will reach retirement age in the coming decade; at other institutions none of the current faculty members will reach age 70 for 20 years. There are institutions at which more than one-half of the retiring faculty do so at the mandatory retirement age of 70 and institutions at which faculty have consistently chosen to retire by age 65. Therefore, the committee cannot predict the effects of eliminating mandatory retirement at each of more than 3,200 colleges and universities.

A college or university that is trying to plan for uncapping cannot rely primarily on the available aggregate data on faculty age distribution and retirement behavior. Yet we found only a few administrators and faculty who had studied their institution's faculty age distributions, retirement patterns, hiring needs, and costs as a way of understanding how their institution would be affected by the elimination of mandatory retirement. Most had not reviewed faculty handbooks, benefits procedures, or retirement programs to consider whether uncapping would require any revisions of college or university policy. The committee thus concludes: **Administrators and faculty can best assess the potential impact of uncapping at their**

**own colleges and universities by studying their faculty age distributions, retirement patterns, and hiring needs in order to estimate the potential effect of uncapping.**

At most colleges and universities, planning will not require the establishment of committees or a long-term study. Retirement patterns alone can indicate whether the elimination of mandatory retirement will have any effect on an institution. For example, prior to 1982 several faculty at one of our case study liberal arts colleges retired after age 70, but since that time faculty members have retired at earlier ages, and most current faculty members report that they plan to retire before age 65. The committee recognizes that analyzing data on faculty ages and retirement patterns is more complicated at colleges and universities with a larger faculty and, in some cases, multiple campuses than at a liberal arts college. Models like those we used in estimating effects on faculty turnover and salary budgets could assist administrators at these colleges and universities in estimating whether faculty are likely to choose to work past age 70.

Moreover, colleges, universities, higher education researchers, and groups representing higher education should all continue to monitor faculty retirements for changes in historical patterns. (We consider the current availability of resources for doing this in our discussion of faculty data bases in Appendix B.) We urge higher education systems and organizations to undertake their own monitoring and planning efforts.

We have expressed serious concern that some research universities will have fewer opportunities to hire and will face additional costs as a result of postponed retirements if mandatory retirement is eliminated. Other colleges and universities may also face low expected faculty turnover for the next decade or more, regardless of mandatory retirement policy, if their faculty age distributions reflect the national distribution with a disproportionately large number of faculty in the middle age ranges. In Chapter 3 we consider whether an increasing proportion of older faculty and decreased hiring opportunities will harm the quality of affected colleges and universities. In that chapter and in Chapters 4 and 5, we consider whether colleges and universities will be able to mitigate any adverse effects of postponed retirements or reduced faculty turnover.

# 3

# Faculty Performance and
# Institutional Quality

An increasing proportion of faculty members over age 70 or of older faculty in general could have adverse effects on colleges and universities for two reasons: Older faculty could be less productive—in scholarship, teaching, and service—because of the effects of aging, and even if older faculty continue to teach and engage in scholarship, reduced turnover because of postponed retirements could limit an institution's ability to hire faculty in new research and teaching fields.

At one level the link between faculty productivity and institutional quality is obvious. The quality of a college or university depends to a large degree on its faculty's work, although the nature of that work varies by an institution's relative emphasis on a range of roles—undergraduate teaching, research, and the training of future scholars (see Appendix C). Institutional quality will decline if the overall quality or quantity of faculty work declines. Moreover, the standards of a discipline can change as new research areas and methods develop, or the standards of a college or university can change as it chooses to emphasize one field over another or to change its balance of research and teaching. Even if a faculty member continues to do excellent work in a particular field, such work may not meet changed standards. Low turnover could hinder the efforts of colleges and universities to improve their quality or to launch new research areas by hiring junior or senior faculty.

In this chapter we examine the effects of age on faculty performance in order to address the question of whether an increased proportion of older faculty members would adversely affect institutional quality. We also evaluate ways colleges and universities can mitigate negative effects on institutional quality and can positively influence individual faculty performance. These options include the use of performance evaluation in combination with actions ranging from administrative and peer feedback to dismissal of incompetent faculty. Finally, we explore the implications of our findings for tenure and for the ability of colleges and universities to maintain or raise institutional quality.

## EFFECTS OF AGE ON PERFORMANCE

### Overall Abilities and Age

Studies suggest that certain abilities decline with age, but not necessarily those central to faculty quality. For example, physical vigor declines with age, as do some physical abilities. Older people typically have more difficulty hearing speech (National Research Council, 1987a). Visual acuity, range of focus, and color discrimination decrease after age 40, although differences among individuals are considerable (National Research Council, 1987b). Some mental abilities may also decline with age. In one study, for example, older people scored lower on certain tests of creativity (Ruth and Birren, 1985); however, people aged 25-35 differed from people aged 45-55 more than those aged 45-55 differed from those aged 65-75. Using a test measuring such skills as remembering an address or reasoning by analogy, a Harvard research team tested for cognitive decline in more than 1,000 healthy volunteer physicians. Although the average total test scores and scores on subtests declined with increasing age, "many functions did not show significant declines up to the age of 65 and for some of the [sub]tests, these changes were not apparent until the age of 75" (Weintraub et al., 1991:6).

Warner Schaie's studies of the relationship between cognitive abilities and age suggest that people of different ages score differently on tests for different types of cognitive ability, which could indicate that certain mental abilities are stronger at certain ages. Younger people score higher on tests requiring quick responses on test questions not related to daily living; older people score higher on tests with questions about legal terms in common contracts and the need to get help from other people (Schaie and Willis, 1986:281). Older people's greater experience with various activities may counteract or compensate for abilities that decline with age (National Research Council, 1990a:26).

Most studies of age and ability compare the abilities of younger and older people, rather than measuring changes over time in the abilities of a single group of people. Therefore, it is impossible for these studies to separate out decreased ability owing to age from any differences owing to other factors, such as the older group's having attended school in a different period. From a policy perspective the distinction may not matter (Bayer and Dutton, 1977:10); if older people now are less able than younger people now, older people will be less desirable employees. However, isolating the effects of aging does matter for the purpose of predicting changes in the performance of individuals who may postpone retirement. The few available studies of groups of people over time suggest little decline in mental ability until age 60, after which the decline is slight until the middle 70s with the rate of decline possibly increasing again in the early 80s (Schaie and Willis, 1986:299). After a series of studies designed to check the validity of the test and the effects of factors other than age that might affect test performance, including different intellectual abilities and medical histories, the Harvard researchers concluded that "normal aging does not entail general mental deterioration. Normal cognitive loss is not broad and debilitating" (Powell, 1991:2). A 7-year study of older people aging from 60 to 67, from 67 to 74, and from 74 to 81 found that there was a decline in the abilities of approximately 30 percent of the people in the younger two categories and 40 percent of the people in the oldest category. Interestingly, there was an improvement in the abilities of approximately 10 percent of the people in all three age categories (Schaie and Willis, 1986:306-307). This evidence suggests there would be little overall decrease in the mental abilities of faculty for several years of continued employment past age 70. Weintraub et al. (1991:4) found that ". . . there are, in fact, individuals over the age of 75 who maintain their cognitive skills at a level overlapping with the average performance of individuals under 35." The variation in individual abilities found in these studies outweighs any general trend of decline with increasing age.

Schaie and Willis point out that the results may be biased by the tendency of less healthy subjects to "drop out" so that decline may begin earlier on average (1986:302-303). But less healthy people may be more likely to retire, and individuals whose cognitive abilities have declined may also be more likely to retire. To test this hypothesis, Weintraub et al. (1991:7) compared the 10 highest and lowest scorers in each age category (over 75 years old, 65-74, 55-64, 45-54, 35-44, and under 35). The top and bottom scorers in the two oldest groups had no statistically significant differences in their medical histories. However, the difference in numbers of top and bottom scorers who were currently working was significant: Of the 20 top scorers aged 65 and over, 12 reported that they continued to work; only 4 of the 20 bottom scorers age 65 and over reported that they continued to work (one participant did not respond to this question).

## Measuring Faculty Performance

The above studies are related to general abilities rather than to the complex range of abilities that make up faculty quality. There are no tests of faculty ability comparable to a vision test or a mental aptitude test. Nevertheless, there have been some studies of the nexus between faculty activities and age.

> Many academics take . . . the "mystical" . . . view of quality in higher education: They maintain that quality simply cannot be defined or measured because the activities of institutions are too complex and varied, because different institutions have different objectives, because the outcomes of higher education are too subtle, because methodological problems are insurmountable, and so on (Astin, 1980:1).

In spite of this widespread view, judgments regarding quality of individuals, departments, and colleges and universities are rendered regularly and depend on the eye of the beholder. For example, rankings of colleges and universities are a common feature of the academic landscape, ranging from rankings of undergraduate programs to rankings of professional schools to periodic studies ranking research doctorate programs by discipline (e.g., Committee on Assessment of Quality-Related Characteristics of Research-Doctorate Programs in the United States, 1982). The bases for such rankings include: purely subjective assessments of reputation and quality; more quantitative counts of faculty publications, student scores, or alumni placement; size of endowment or research funding; and a host of other factors. These measures cannot reflect fully what we mean by quality in higher education, however, nor are they always current. Over time, faculty come and go and departmental reputations rise and fall, prompting periodic reassessments and constant discussions of the relative quality of departments and institutions. Furthermore, measuring faculty quality, like measuring any quality, requires the exercise of values and judgment. Institutional standards as well as disciplinary standards shape the measures of quality for any given institution or department. Consequently, different colleges' and universities' standards of faculty quality must reflect their different priorities and missions.

## Teaching and Age

Studies of teaching ability generally rely on student evaluations of faculty members. The lack of measures of teaching success prevents checking the validity of faculty scores on teacher evaluations, although researchers have checked their reliability. For example, Blackburn and Lawrence (1986:271-272) found that the results of different teaching evaluation instruments are highly correlated (over 0.9):

> When factor analyzed, the same factors emerge. Students take completing the instruments seriously and do not simply randomly fill in the spaces. Test-retest reliabilities are over 0.9. . . . When colleagues also rate a faculty member as to the quality of his or her teaching, the correlations with student ratings are high (around 0.7). . . . The correlations between administrator and student ratings are about 0.5.

However, the tendency of students to give faculty high ratings reduces the spread of scores and weakens statistical relationships between teaching scores and age or any other factor (Blackburn and Lawrence, 1986:272-273).

Studies of faculty at the start of their careers suggest that teaching ratings initially improve with experience. Students give the lowest average teaching ratings to faculty in their first 2 years of teaching (McKeachie, 1983:60). Centra and Creech (1976) found that faculty in their third to twelfth year of teaching earned the highest teaching ratings, but they did not test for differences among faculty with more than 12 years of experience.

Since most studies of the relationship between teaching ability and age are based on student ratings of faculty at one or two institutions, the number of faculty in an age group, particularly the oldest age groups, is so small that an individual exception could mask a trend. The only conclusion one can safely draw from these studies is that they do not show a trend. The results range from showing increasing ratings followed by decreasing ratings for an overall negative correlation between age and teaching ratings (Blackburn and Lawrence, 1986:272-273); to nonsignificant correlations (Blackburn, 1972; Blackburn and Lawrence, 1986:272-273); to teaching ratings at a single university increasing with age for faculty over age 50 in the humanities and 65 or older in the social sciences, but decreasing after age 46 for faculty in the sciences (Kinney and Smith, 1989). On the basis of a study of two liberal arts colleges, Blackburn (1972) found increased variation in teaching scores by age. Although such evidence is hardly conclusive, it does not indicate that the teaching ability of college and university faculty declines with age.

## Research and Age

The question of whether age affects the quality or quantity of an individual's scholarship is an old one. On the basis of data for a sample of scientists, medical researchers, and philosophers who made "significant contributions" based on reviews of histories of science, Lehman (1953) found that most such contributions were made by individuals younger than 45. However, Lehman examined the productivity at different ages only of people who at some age had made a significant contribution, not the proportion of all researchers in each age group who made such a contribution (National Research Council, 1980:207). Thus, his results do not shed light on the probability of a researcher at any given age making a significant contribution or on how the probability of making a significant contribution changes with age.

Direct, quantitative measures of the quality of research are unavailable, and thus there is little evidence on the relationship between age and research quality. Some researchers have measured the scholarly productivity of faculty in general—rather than of the few faculty making major scientific discoveries—by using counts of publications. This approach provides some measure of scholarly activity, although results may be biased by variations in types of publication by age. For example, if older faculty publish more books and fewer articles, their average number of publications may be lower than the average number for younger faculty. Variation in the quality of publications could also affect these results if one age group is more likely to publish in prestigious journals or to be cited by other authors. Over (1989) compared the age distribution of authors of frequently cited articles in psychology journals to the age distribution of authors of less frequently cited articles in the same journals. He found more articles by younger authors but no relationship between age and frequency of citation. If frequency of citation is a measure of an article's influence, this study found no relationship between age and the publication of influential articles.

Studies of quantity of publications vary from counts of articles to counts of all publications with and without weighting for type of publication (e.g., a book equals three articles) and with and without weighting for some measure of prestige (e.g., type of journal or number of times publication cited). The mixed results generally show an initial rise in number of publications, then a more steady output, followed by a decline (Blackburn and Lawrence, 1986:275). Regression analyses of data on approximately 2,000 tenured arts and science faculty in a 1989 Carnegie Foundation survey show an inverse correlation between faculty age and number of professional writings published or accepted for publication over the preceding 2 years. Although older faculty on average published fewer writings than younger faculty, in the sciences and humanities the difference between the average number of writings published by a group of faculty at one age and the number of writings published by the group of faculty 1 year older decreases as age increases (Howe and Smith, 1990:19):

> It should be emphasized that these findings do not suggest that research activity ceases as the faculty member approaches the current mandatory retirement age. They show that between age 60 and age 70, recent publishing activity for the average tenured faculty member would decrease by 0.2 articles [over a decade] in the humanities, by 0.5 articles in the social sciences, and by 0.4 articles in the physical and biological sciences.

Bayer and Dutton (1977) fitted curves to data on number of publications over 2 years and career age from a 1972 American Council on Education survey of faculty for seven disciplines. They found that in six—chemical engineering, earth sciences, economics, experimental psychology, physics, and sociology—the best fit model showed two groups of faculty publishing most: those with approximately 10 years of experience and those with between 30 and 40 years of experience. In biochemistry, faculty with approximately 20 years of career experience published more than faculty with both more and less experience. These patterns suggest that, at least in some disciplines, older faculty may publish as much as or more than their younger colleagues. However, the equations also show no strong relationship between age and quantity of publications.

Furthermore, individual rates of publication vary widely, regardless of age. As an extreme example of individual variance, one study found that in every age group, Nobel laureates published more than a sample of nonlaureates chosen from *American Men of Science* and matched to the laureates by age, field of specialization, and organizational affiliation at the time of the award (university, government, independent nonprofit, or industrial laboratory) (Zuckerman, 1977:145,302).

A study of a single university provided a possible explanation for the higher productivity of the faculty with 30-40 years' experience. Information on the average dollar value of sponsored research support by age for faculty at Stanford University showed a consistent pattern for 1979, 1982, and 1987 (Biedenweg, 1989:32):

> . . . average research [volume, measured in dollars] increases until around age 50, then slowly drops until around age 65, at which point the average starts increasing again. It is believed that self selection [i.e., retirements of faculty less engaged in research] causes the increase for this age group. . . .

In disciplines for which outside funding for research is common, having a research grant can be a predictor of research activity. Howe and Smith (1990) used regression equations on data from the 1989 Carnegie Foundation faculty survey to estimate the effect of age on the probability of having a grant from the federal government, a foundation, or industry for tenured faculty in social science and in biological and physical sciences at 4-year universities. They concluded (Howe and Smith, 1990:22):

> . . . [age] has a [statistically] significant and negative effect on receipt of grant support in both disciplines, though in each case [social science and biological and physical sciences] the effect is quite small. . . . Other factors again [as in predicting number of publications] have a much larger influence on the probability of receiving major grant support.

The cause of the inverse relationship between grant-getting and age from these data cannot be determined (Howe and Smith, 1990:21):

> [B]ecause there is no information on grant applications, no consideration can be given to differences by age in the propensity to seek outside support for research. Finally, it must be acknowledged that a decline in the probability of grant support with age, may, in part, reflect age discrimination by the funding institutions and not be wholly attributable to a decline in either research activity or research quality with age.

The National Science Foundation does not keep information on the age of applicants for its grants, but it found (1988:4) that "21 percent of applicants had received their highest degree since 1980, 41 percent received it between 1970 and 1979, 26 percent between 1960 and 1969, and 11 percent before 1960."

One of our case study universities obtained 1979 and 1985 data from the National Institute of Health (NIH) on applicants' success rates by age in receiving new grants and renewing old grants. For grant applicants who reported their date of birth, those aged 31-50 had a higher probability of getting a grant than those aged 51-70. However, when the data are divided into 5-year age groups, the probabilities for applicants over 50 do not show a clear or steady trend of decline with age. The committee obtained NIH data on numbers of research grant holders by date of birth for 1987 and 1989, reported in Table 5. However, the NIH data do not show clear evidence of declining research interest with age, since the number of active faculty born before 1925 is probably small.

In general, administrators support new research areas by hiring new faculty. They regard new positions as an opportunity to define the future of a department. New positions, however, do not necessarily demand younger faculty. Limited evidence indicates that age is only one of the factors affecting which scholars work in new research areas. Based on a study of 96 geologists' responses to plate tectonics, Messeri (1988) concluded that receptivity to new ideas and willingness to engage in research based on new theories depends on professional standing as well as age. Zuckerman (1988:68) summarized these findings: "[I]t was largely the middle-aged and compara- tively well-established scientists who adopted these ideas while they [were] still controversial and speculative; younger scientists followed only after the research potentials of these ideas had become clear." In contrast, Hull, Tessner, and Diamond (1978) found that in the nineteenth century, younger

TABLE 5   National Institutes of Health Research Grant Holders, by Year of Birth, 1987 and 1989

| Year of Birth | Percentage of Grant Holders | |
|---|---|---|
| | In 1987 | In 1989 |
| After 1955 | 1 | 4 |
| 1946-1955 | 33 | 24 |
| 1936-1945 | 32 | 20 |
| 1926-1935 | 14 | 22 |
| Before 1925 | 5 | 7 |
| Not reported | 14 | 22 |

*Source:* Data provided by National Institutes of Health.

natural scientists accepted Darwinian theory more readily than older scientists, and scientists past middle age predominated among the few who resisted Darwinian theory for more than a decade.

The evidence on age and new research fields is not of sufficient depth or clarity to draw firm conclusions. We believe that the process of developing new research fields involves complex interactions among professional and scientific variables, of which age is only one factor. This complexity may be reflected in the varied patterns of hiring in higher education: some colleges and universities prefer to hire junior faculty; others renew their faculty and enter new research areas primarily by bringing in middle-aged senior faculty with the professional standing to confidently adopt and pursue new ideas.

## Changing Interests and Age

Faculty activities may vary by age less because of changing abilities than because of changing interests. However, research in this area is inconclusive in that one cannot separate the effects of aging from other factors. For example, a study of male faculty from 12 midwestern liberal arts colleges, at career stages ranging from new assistant professors to "full professors within five years of formal retirement" found that self-reported "comfortableness with teaching" increased for each succeeding career group, while comfortableness with research and scholarship was lowest for full professors (Baldwin and Blackburn, 1981:605). The 1989 Carnegie Foundation survey of faculty found the percentage of faculty identifying their interests as "primarily in research" or "leaning toward research" was highest for faculty under age 40 and lowest for faculty aged 60-64, while the percentages of faculty interested "primarily in teaching" showed the reverse trend. These results may be due to differences between generations rather than effects of age. Of greater interest, the percentage of faculty preferring research is higher among faculty aged 65 and older than among faculty aged 60-64 (Carnegie Foundation for the Advancement of Teaching, 1989:43), supporting the hypothesis that faculty engaged in research are more likely to retire later.

Through its letters of inquiry and case studies, the committee heard from both faculty and administrators that many faculty are able to make continuing contributions regardless of age, that the older generation has something special to contribute, and that declines in faculty performance can occur at any age.

> During this time my personal observation has been that there have been many members of the faculty doing an excellent job teaching well into their sixties and seventies (faculty senate chair).

I have found older professors very capable of stimulating younger faculty members.  There is much that the older generation can contribute to the development of the younger generation of professors (college president).

A faculty member is not "dead wood" just because he has lived a long time; many people retire mentally when they are rather young (college president).

Midcareer faculty may become less active scholars or less capable teachers as a result of getting stuck in a line of research inquiry or a particular approach in the classroom.  As Corcoran and Clark (1989:27) note: "[I]t is easy to imagine that jadedness could set in after years of teaching routine courses in the curriculum, and that older faculty could feel far removed from the cutting edge of a rapidly changing field (biology, for example)." This factor could account for the declining performance of some older faculty, but getting stuck in a rut is not a function of age.  An example may help to clarify the distinction between effects of time and effects of age: Assume that faculty produce poorer research at the end of 10 years of studying a single narrow area or that faculty are poorer teachers at the end of 10 years teaching the same material.  A line of inquiry could be pursued to its conclusion and exhausted, the results of a study could be fully accounted for, or a syllabus could fail to reflect important recent developments in a field.  This can be true whether the faculty start the research or teaching in question at age 30, 40, or 60.  Based on a study of faculty at one "research-oriented university," Corcoran and Clark (1989:27) conclude "that stuckness or work blockage is not an exceptional experience for faculty members at any stage of their lives."

## Conclusions

On the basis of our review of the literature, as well as our experience, it is clear that measures of research activity show no strong relationship with age. Moreover, studies have not shown a clear decline of teaching ability with advancing age.  In scholarship and in teaching, individual variance is greater than any average tendencies to decline.  An older faculty member who performs less well than he or she did a decade earlier may nevertheless perform at a higher level than a colleague a decade or more younger and thereby contribute as much or more to an institution's reputation for quality.

In some cases performance may decline because a faculty member falls into patterns of poor teaching and uninspired scholarship.  The committee believes many of these cases have been mistakenly attributed to inevitable age-related declines. Therefore, in the next section we address ways faculty and administrators can respond to declining faculty performance.

Although there is little evidence in the literature on aging and responsiveness to new developments in a field, evidence from our letter survey and case studies indicates that colleges and universities rely on hiring as a way of supporting new areas of research and teaching. The committee is thus deeply concerned about colleges' and universities' need for new (not necessarily young) faculty members as bearers of new ideas and research areas. We address policies that affect faculty turnover in Chapter 4 and policies specifically designed to encourage faculty turnover in Chapter 5.

## EVALUATION OF FACULTY MEMBERS

Some faculty and administrators have raised the question of whether colleges and universities can accurately measure the performance of tenured faculty members. They have also questioned whether faculty development or dismissal could provide an effective way of maintaining faculty and institutional quality. Lastly, some have questioned whether evaluating tenured faculty threatens tenure and collegiality. In this section we review ways of evaluating the performance of individuals in academia and other settings and possible actions based on the results of faculty evaluation.

As detailed above, there is no precise way to measure faculty performance. Moreover, studies of personnel evaluation instruments in industry and government (National Research Council, 1991:3) show that although performance appraisal may be justified as a way to provide employees with feedback on their actions and to motivate them, it cannot be justified on the basis of scientific validity. Effective job performance is difficult to describe or observe for the purposes of measurement, particularly in the case of professional and managerial jobs in which people have a higher degree of autonomy in setting job goals and activities. Definitions of effectiveness are subjective and vary over time. It would be possible to improve the reliability and validity of existing performance appraisal measures, but one comprehensive review of the research literature on performance appraisal in industry and government concluded that in the case of appraising federal managers, "vast human and financial resources" would be required to develop performance appraisal instruments meeting "the strictest challenges of measurement science." Instead, the committee concluded that for most personnel management decisions, ". . . the goal of a performance appraisal should be to support and encourage informed managerial judgment, and not to aspire to the degree of standardization, precision, and empirical support that would be required of, for example, selection tests." Likewise, in the absence of reliable and valid selection tests, colleges and universities cannot use performance appraisal as any kind of scientifically accurate basis for identifying nonperforming faculty or even faculty who are performing less well than some of their peers.

Despite the lack of scientific measures, colleges, universities, industry, and governments all use various procedures and practices to evaluate their employees. Many use evaluations to give feedback to employees about their performance. Academia has a long tradition of evaluating faculty carefully and acting on evaluations through the process of promotion and granting tenure. Depending on the purpose, colleges and universities place different emphasis on different kinds of evaluations and the actions that are based on those evaluations. Bryant Kearl, cited in Reisman (1986:75-76), lists common areas of faculty evaluation:

• public scrutiny of professors' ideas as these are regularly presented in lectures and writing;
• reviews of faculty applications for research grants or awards for study or travel;
• student evaluations of teaching;
• promotional reviews of tenured associate professors considered for full professorships;
• recommendations for annual salary increments;
• decisions about university teaching awards and allocation of named professorships or chairs;
• departmental reviews in which note is taken of functioning of individual faculty; and
• review of articles and book manuscripts submitted for publication.

Of course, evaluation practices vary among institutions and among departments within institutions. Some institutions and departments use formal written evaluations; many do not. Colleges and universities with faculty collective bargaining agreements may have to have contractual arrangements for faculty evaluation. Some colleges and universities rely more heavily than others on peer review in faculty evaluation. A few use peer review in conjunction with decisions about salaries, sabbaticals, and internally allocated research funds. Many use peer review only as a part of major personnel actions, such as promotion to tenure or to full professor and dismissal proceedings.

Regardless of its use, formal evaluation of tenured faculty remains controversial. When the National Commission on Higher Education Issues recommended formal evaluation of tenured faculty, Committee A on Academic Freedom and Tenure (American Association of University Professors, 1983:14a) responded:

> The Association believes that periodic formal institutional evaluation of each postprobationary faculty member would bring scant benefit, would incur unacceptable costs, not only in money and time but also in a dampening of creativity and collegial relationships, and would threaten academic freedom.

Some colleges and universities have reduced the perceived threat of formal evaluation by not confining it to use in the faculty dismissal process. A review of faculty development programs in Minnesota and North and South Dakota (Eble and McKeachie, 1985:217) found:

> [the most successful programs] did not aim at "deadwood" or "developing" those who had been ineffective but rather offered opportunities for the solid, substantial contributors as well as the "stars" or the alienated; they gave the faculty the sense that they were valued.

Other reviews of evaluation and feedback programs at colleges and universities also suggest the potential of these programs. Centra (1978:34) found that a combination of students' teaching evaluations and self-evaluations led teachers whose student ratings were lower than their self-assessments to change their teaching techniques:

> These changes were most evident in the instructors' preparation for class, use of class time, summarization of major points in lectures and discussions, openness to other viewpoints, and the likelihood of making helpful comments on papers and exams.

A few colleges and universities have adopted extensive processes for evaluating tenured faculty (Goodman, 1990; Licata, 1985, 1986). The University of California system uses departmental committee reviews of assistant and associate professors every 2 years and of full professors every 3 years as a basis for salary reviews and promotions. Reviews for major promotions involve campus-wide review committees and external review letters. At one of our case study universities, department chairs review the annual report from each member of the department and rate each as satisfactory, meriting official concern, or inadequate. The department chair, sometimes with the assistance of other faculty members, meets with tenured faculty members who receive less than satisfactory evaluations to develop a plan for improvement, which can involve such redirection of effort as a greater teaching load for a faculty member who is doing little research or suggestions on how to improve the faculty member's current efforts. Another case study research university has just implemented a similar procedure, with the stipulation that at least three senior faculty members advise the chair or dean of a department in assessing an individual's performance and in developing a plan for improvement if the individual disagrees with the chair's initial assessment.

Formal and regular evaluation processes require commitment on the part of both faculty and administrators. At one case study university, the arts and sciences dean meets with each department chair, going over the annual reports submitted by all tenure track and tenured faculty in the department and grading each one on research, teaching, and service in connection with the awarding of merit raises. The provost reported that annual review of 600 faculty takes "a brutal amount of time" but added that the faculty members must spend several hours filling out the reports, so "we owe it to them" to give the reports careful consideration. The dean has found that a systematic process of faculty evaluation is also useful for purposes as wide-ranging as awarding a teaching prize to finding evidence in a lawsuit alleging discriminatory awarding of raises.

For some colleges and universities the time and resources required for an elaborate formal evaluation procedure may outweigh the benefits. "Formal, precise performance appraisals" of employees whose performance is not easily quantified and measured "may make employees skeptical of their performance appraisals" (National Research Council, 1991:133). Faculty and administrators at some colleges and universities have found that less formal reviews can also provide the basis for feedback, ranging from rewards to notices that an individual's current activities are unlikely to result in rewards. At one of our case study liberal arts colleges, the dean of the faculty informally follows the progress of faculty members. Several faculty reported that they expected the dean and their colleagues to let them know if their performance declined.

Measures of individual faculty performance and of faculty quality in general need to be broad enough to fit different institutional missions and the different roles faculty play. Clark, Corcoran, and Lewis (1986:178) state:

> . . . ideal types of faculty and faculty performance emphases will differ according to institutional type and mission. Institutions that emphasize teaching and/or service will need to focus more on faculty development policies that revitalize routine teaching and retrain faculty for shifting curricular emphases, whereas institutions that emphasize the research and scholarly orientation will need to consider more attentively the adequacy of sponsorship and resources to sustain scholarly productivity.

Standards can also recognize different individual activities within an institution. A committee of faculty and administrators reviewing the need for evaluation procedures for one division of a state university suggested a lower standard of research productivity for faculty who are serving in administrative positions or who have just completed administrative service (Faculty Development and Renewal Subcommittee, 1987). Colleges and universities can seek to maintain overall faculty quality by assigning faculty members, when possible, in ways that meet institutional needs. As noted above, one university assigns additional teaching to some faculty members who are less active in research. Periodic review of faculty assignments provides a way of recognizing that faculty interests and abilities may change over time. However, recognizing changes in individual interests and trying to match individual activities and institutional goals do not offer a complete solution to divergence between individual and institutional goals. More faculty members may want to emphasize research, teaching, or service than an institution needs.

Evaluations can be used to give faculty feedback on both the quality of their work and how their activities fit disciplinary and institutional directions. **The committee concludes that faculty performance evaluation can be a useful tool for maintaining and improving faculty quality, particularly when administrators and faculty use it to provide faculty with feedback on their performance.**

**The committee recommends that faculty and administrators at all colleges and universities work to develop ways to offer faculty feedback on their performance.**

We recognize that institutional goals, standards, and governance vary, and, consequently, different ways will be appropriate at different colleges and universities. We believe elaborate systems for faculty review may not be worth the additional effort and cost.

We stress that faculty should play a role in providing colleagues with feedback on their performance. Traditions of academic freedom and collegiality limit outside control over a faculty member's activities, but the committee believes faculty and administrators can find collegial, informal, and positive ways to assist some faculty who get stuck in unproductive scholarship or teaching.

## THE EXTREME CASES: FACULTY DISMISSAL

Not all faculty will respond positively to efforts at faculty development. In this section we consider the dismissal of tenured faculty in response to concerns about both individual and institutional quality.

Negative evaluations rarely lead to dismissals. In our contacts with colleges and universities, including our 17 case studies, we heard of almost no cases of dismissal for nonperformance. The formal evaluation processes cited above include as a possible outcome the start of procedures leading to dismissal, but colleges and universities keep procedures leading to dismissal separate from evaluation and development, and they rarely resort to them.

The primary barriers to the dismissal of faculty for nonperformance are traditions of collegiality and the administrative difficulty of dismissal. Many faculty members and a few administrators at our case study institutions stated that they would rather have their institution carry the weight of the occasional inadequate faculty member than risk a dismissal that might undermine the principle of tenure protecting all faculty members. Although the 1940 Statement of Principles on Academic Freedom and Tenure set the guiding principles behind most institutional tenure policies and practices, the definition of tenure, its legal basis, and the procedures to be followed in dismissal cases vary widely among colleges and universities and sometimes even within divisions of an institution (Commission on Academic Tenure in Higher Education, 1973:2-3).  The courts that have reviewed cases of faculty dismissal have recognized that colleges and universities have the right to dismiss tenured faculty members.  The 1973 Commission on Academic Tenure in Higher Education, jointly sponsored by the Association of American Colleges and the American Association of University Professors, recommended (Commission on Academic Tenure in Higher Education, 1973:75): ". . . 'adequate cause' in faculty dismissal proceedings should be restricted to (a) demonstrated incompetency or dishonesty, (b) substantial and manifest neglect of duty, and (c) personal conduct which substantially impairs the individual's fulfillment of his institutional responsibilities."

Courts have upheld the dismissal of faculty for causes ranging from refusal to teach an assigned course to failure to meet classes on a regular basis and to demonstrated unfamiliarity with the basic concepts of the subject matter taught (Morris, 1990).  In general, they have held that tenure provides a presumption of professional competence but not a right to lifetime employment.  Morris (1990:15) concludes:  "[T]enure's procedural requirement of full academic due process only guarantees basic procedural fairness by the institution when dealing with faculty members about quite important concerns, such as dismissal."

Dismissing faculty would remain difficult even in the absence of tenure.  Some colleges and universities with faculty collective bargaining agreements have contractual limits to their ability to dismiss faculty in addition to the traditional protection provided by tenure.  Moreover, if colleges and universities began to hire faculty under contracts with a fixed term instead of tenure, regular contract renewals could require more regular faculty performance appraisal; disproportionate nonrenewal of the contracts of older faculty would raise questions of age discrimination (Finkin, 1989).

Anecdotal evidence suggests that in institutions of higher education—as in business or other organizations—administrators can take steps leading to the resignation or retirement of a nonperforming employee without completing a formal dismissal procedure.  In some cases the suggestion of possible dismissal proceedings has prompted a faculty member to leave, or a faculty member has left before procedures leading to dismissal were complete.  In other cases administrators and a faculty member negotiate arrangements for the individual's departure without mention of dismissal (see discussion of ad hoc individual buyouts in Chapter 4).  Such arrangements can benefit both the faculty member and the institution:  The individual departs without the stigma of having been dismissed, administrators and colleagues do not have to expend the effort required to dismiss a faculty member with due process, and the institution avoids the effects of a dismissal on collegiality and morale. However, quiet dismissals could also deprive faculty members of due process that might have ended in a decision not to dismiss. Since departures of nonperforming faculty by means other than formal dismissal are not recorded, there is no evidence on the frequency or fairness of such procedures.

Evidence from a review of cases on the dismissal of tenured faculty gives some guidance as to fair and acceptable procedures for dealing with poorly performing faculty, whether the case eventually leads to dismissal or not. Although the procedures vary from institution to institution, dismissing a faculty member generally requires administrative effort in assembling and reviewing evidence. Since review by colleagues is the traditional basis for judging faculty quality, performance appraisals for dismissal also usually include peer review. Due process requires that administrators give to an individual considered for dismissal notice and opportunities to respond, in some cases including opportunities for improvement and development during a probationary period prior to the beginning of formal dismissal procedures (Morris, 1990).

The actual amount of effort required to dismiss a tenured faculty member varies from case to case, depending on institutional policy, the nature of the case, and the individual administrators and faculty involved. However, our discussions with faculty and administrators led us to conclude that in all cases these procedures impose significant costs to faculty and administrative time, create potential legal expenses, and cause considerable strain on faculty and administrative morale. Although the formal dismissal of tenured faculty and resignations of faculty in lieu of dismissal do provide colleges and universities with a means of responding to individual performance problems, these means are designed for infrequent use in the worst cases, not as a general solution to coping with changing faculty performance.

Colleges and universities can dismiss tenured faculty members in response to extreme financial problems. Colleges and universities can also dismiss tenured faculty when, acting in good faith, they close a department or program and the tenured faculty in that department or program cannot be reassigned. However, the ability of colleges and universities to close departments or dismiss faculty in response to what is legally termed "financial exigency" is not likely to be relevant to problems arising specifically from the end of mandatory retirement. There are a number of "substantive technical, bureaucratic, and emotional barriers" to closing academic programs, including adverse effects on faculty morale (Mortimer, Bagshaw, and Masland, 1985:51-53).

Some medical schools raised a particular financial concern. At many medical schools tenured faculty are expected to "earn" a large proportion of their salaries from outside funds. (This is distinct from the common practice of allowing a faculty member whose work is supported by an outside grant to use such funds to cover a salary reduction in order to teach less and devote more time to research.)  Some medical schools interpret tenure as a guarantee of a salary based on expected outside earnings, and faculty and administrators at those schools have expressed concern that older faculty members would obtain fewer grants or see fewer patients and become a burden on the school budget.  However, most medical schools define a base salary protected by tenure and exclude income from research grants or clinical practice from the base amount.  Our analysis of tenure law suggests that grant and clinical practice income are not part of salary protected by tenure as long as university rules specify this (Morris, 1990).  We believe universities should define the link between tenure and salary to exclude or limit outside income above a base salary protected by tenure.

At the beginning of this chapter, we distinguished between poor faculty performance resulting from (1) declining productivity because of age and (2) work that may have been consistent with previous disciplinary or institutional standards but that limits an institution's ability to upgrade.  In the first instance, an increase in the number of faculty over age 70 or, more generally, an increase in the average age of faculty does not necessarily affect institutional quality.  Studies of the relationship between age and cognitive abilities, teaching ratings, and research activity suggest faculty can continue to perform well in their 70s and that there are variations in performance among faculty of any age.  Moreover, there is little evidence on whether the number of inadequate faculty would increase if faculty were allowed to work past age 70; some evidence suggests that poor performers may be less likely to keep working past age 65.  Therefore, dismissal of faculty members for poor performance is rare now and likely to remain rare. Dismissal procedures are intended for rare extreme cases, not regular use.

The second possibility is more troublesome because it does not necessarily involve a decline in individual productivity, and if it happens to a number of faculty members, the quality of the institution or the department can be harmed.  Moreover, it can happen to a faculty member well before age 70. Consequently, mandatory retirement does not directly address these problems.

Tenure does not protect faculty against dismissal for inadequate performance.  Colleges and universities can dismiss tenured faculty for adequate cause provided they afford due process in a clearly defined and understood dismissal procedure. Therefore, the committee concludes:  **Eliminating mandatory retirement would not pose a threat to tenure.**

Performance evaluation followed by dismissal of poor performers is not a necessary or useful response to the elimination of mandatory retirement. Colleges and universities hoping to hire scholars in new fields or to change the balance of faculty research and teaching interests will need to look to mechanisms other than dismissal for encouraging turnover.  We address mechanisms associated with pensions and other retirement programs in the next two chapters.

# 4

# Pensions, Retirement Programs, and Costs

Faculty near retirement are concerned not only about receiving an adequate pension income and health care insurance (Gray, 1989; Mulanaphy, 1984) but also about losing contact with their colleagues, students, institution, and academic field (see, e.g., Daniels and Daniels, 1990b; Felicetti, 1982). Some administrators and faculty have expressed concern that faculty may postpone retirement if they are uncertain about provision for financial, scholarly, or collegial needs.

The idea that colleges and universities should respond to these needs is not a new one. Harvard President Charles Eliot defined the goals of a faculty pension program when proposing the nation's first private university "Retiring Allowance Fund" in 1879:

> First, it would add to the dignity and attractiveness of the service, by securing all participants against the chance of falling into poverty late in life, or of seeing an associate so reduced; secondly, it would provide for participants the means of honorable ease, when the capacity and the inclination for work abate.

The Carnegie Foundation for the Advancement of Teaching established the Teachers Insurance Annuity Association (TIAA) in 1937 to administer a pension program for faculty at colleges and universities nationwide. The tradition of recognizing an affiliation between retired faculty and institutions is even older; the position of emeritus professor dates back at least to the early nineteenth century.

Colleges and universities need to balance the goal of providing for retired faculty with other objectives: preserving hiring opportunities, developing the ability to predict and plan for those opportunities, and controlling scarce resources. As noted in Chapter 2, some institutions will face increased costs and decreased hiring opportunities if mandatory retirement is eliminated. Economic conditions and employment, benefit, and discrimination law limit an institution's ability to respond to potential effects of eliminating mandatory retirement. The committee has two additional goals that guided its assessment of retirement benefit programs. First, we believe retirement benefit programs should create neither incentives to continue working nor disincentives to retirement: That is, we believe faculty retirement decisions should depend primarily on factors other than financial concerns. Second, we believe any changes a college or university makes in its retirement benefit policies should be within the bounds of its current faculty compensation budget. The committee recognizes that colleges and universities have limited sources of additional revenue, and we have sought ways to limit potential expenses created by the elimination of mandatory retirement.

In this chapter the committee examines how administrators, faculty, and collective bargaining units can analyze and, if necessary, adjust faculty retirement benefit policies in order to meet both institutional needs for turnover and individual needs for retirement security. We first examine the effects on faculty retirement of two standard employee benefits: pensions and health care. We then examine two other retirement benefit options: continued faculty perquisites and retirement planning assistance. Throughout, we consider whether colleges and universities could use retirement benefit policies and programs to mitigate the projected negative effects of uncapping, that is, decreased hiring opportunities and increased costs.

## PENSIONS

### Goals

The Commission on College Retirement (1990:168) stated goals for a faculty pension plan:

> *First,* a pension plan should provide income for the lifetimes of the retirees and their spouses. . . .
> *Second,* a pension plan should provide income that, when added to other sources of support available to the family, can be expected to maintain throughout retirement a standard of living comparable to that enjoyed immediately prior to retirement.

As the commission's second goal suggests, retirement income can be measured by the extent to which it supports a pensioner's preretirement standard of living. Pension plans have traditionally been designed to provide retirees with an income that, when added to Social Security income, is equal to a proportion of their preretirement income by an expected retirement age. In the absence of special circumstances, such as poor health, retirees generally face fewer expenses than employees. Therefore, the proportion of preretirement income a retiree needs to maintain his or her preretirement standard of living is usually less than 100 percent (Commission on College Retirement, 1990). (We discuss the issue of retiree health coverage later in this chapter.) A 1988 amendment to the joint "Statement of Principles on Academic Retirement and Insurance Plans" of the Association of American Colleges and the American Association of University Professors recommends that retirement income from pensions, Social Security, and any other sources should provide continuing purchasing power equivalent to at least two-thirds of preretirement income. The committee accepts this definition of minimum adequacy, and our recommendations are based on that acceptance.

**The committee recommends that universities and colleges offer pension plans designed to provide retirees with a continuing (i.e., adjusted for inflation) retirement income from all sources equal to at least 67 percent of their preretirement income.**

In addition, we suggest that institutions set a maximum target for continuing pension income in the interest of best allocating scarce institutional resources and limiting inadvertent incentives to postpone retirement. We found that faculty at some universities with generous pension plans could increase their annual pension income by 10-14 percent, or several thousand dollars, by postponing retirement for 1 year (see Table 6 and discussion below). Colleges and universities could redirect any funds saved by limiting institutional pension contributions to other benefits for retired faculty, such as health care benefits and programs for retirees.

**The committee recommends that universities and colleges offer pension plans designed to provide retirees with a continuing retirement income from all sources equal to no more than 100 percent of their preretirement income.**

The committee's recommended pension income range calls for a *continuing* level of income (i.e., an income that continues to be equal to 67-100 percent of preretirement income in real terms), not just an initial level. Faculty are concerned not only about the level of income they will receive when they retire but also about whether inflation will erode that income over time. Inflation has seriously eroded pension incomes in the past, and we therefore recommend a range of pension incomes only when incomes in that range can be protected against inflation. Colleges and universities cannot meet the goal of providing for their retired faculty without protecting pensions against inflation. (We discuss ways of protecting pensions against inflation later in this section.) Moreover, worry about inflation may lead faculty to retire later than they would otherwise choose to do.

In recommending goals for pension contribution policies, we refer to income from all sources, so our recommendation depends in part on levels of Social Security income, and, for many faculty, it will depend on pensions from more than one institution. We have recommended that colleges and universities design institutional and, when applicable, faculty contributions to pension plans that will provide the difference between Social Security and 67-100 percent of preretirement income. Some colleges and universities already use programs such as matching employee pension contributions as a way to encourage saving for retirement. Of course, actual pension incomes vary, depending on institutional policies and market performance. In some cases faculty can choose to place their retirement contributions into investments with different rates of return, so an individual faculty member's pension will depend on his or her investment choices. Individual pensions may be based on employment at more than one institution or outside academia. Therefore, our recommendation proposes upper and lower bounds to guide pension contribution policies rather than a single target percentage of preretirement income.

## Types of Pension Plans

Various researchers (e.g., Daniels and Daniels, 1990a; Lozier and Dooris, 1990) have estimated the number of faculty members covered by different types of pension plan, but not all pension plan providers or colleges and universities separate faculty from other employees in their pension records. In addition, approximately 11 percent of all colleges and universities offer faculty a choice of pension plan types (Daniels and Daniels, 1990a:7). Therefore, precise figures on the number of faculty covered by different types of plan cannot be calculated. Because the details of pension plans vary across the more than 3,200 colleges and universities in the country, we can only discuss general pension plan characteristics. Likewise, because the pension of any individual faculty member can be based on service at several colleges and universities and, in some cases, employment outside academia, disincentives to retirement and the level of financial reward for continued employment vary from individual to individual as well as from institution to institution. Approximately 6 percent of 4-year colleges and universities do not offer pension plans other than Social Security; they employ less than 1 percent of all faculty (Daniels and Daniels, 1990a:1).

The two major types of pension plans provided by colleges and universities in the United States are defined contribution plans and defined benefit plans. Two other plan types exist: hybrid plans—some of which have been designed to limit financial incentives to postpone retirement—and target benefit plans, but they are rare in higher education.

## Defined Contribution Plans

Defined contribution plans typically specify that the institution will set aside a percentage of a faculty member's salary to be invested in a pension fund account for the faculty member. In addition, faculty members can usually contribute up to some specified additional percentage from their own pretax earnings; in many cases they are required to do so. The pension fund may offer faculty members a choice of investment options, such as money market, stocks, bonds, or a combination of these. The faculty member, not the college or university, owns the accumulation and bears the investment risk. The college or university guarantees only to contribute its portion of the faculty member's salary, not to provide a fixed level of retirement income.

On retirement, participants in defined contribution plans receive an annuity that is based on the amount contributed over the years, the accumulated earnings or appreciation (in the case of stock funds) of those contributions, and an actuarial calculation based on life expectancy. The pension fund may offer the faculty member a choice of ways to receive the income, with annuity designs that vary to adjust for expected inflation; to provide for a spouse or other dependents; or, in some cases, to allow the retiree to collect a lump-sum payment.

Approximately 75 percent of 4-year U.S. colleges and universities offer defined contribution plans (Daniels and Daniels, 1990a:7). Most private colleges and universities offer this type of plan. The percentage of faculty covered by defined contribution plans is less than 75 percent because, on average, private institutions have fewer faculty than public institutions. Defined contribution plans are usually managed by private insurers, the largest of which is the Teachers Annuity and Assurance Association-College Retirement Equities Fund (TIAA-CREF). TIAA-CREF was established in part to protect pensions from the effects of faculty mobility. Because faculty members in defined contribution plans own their accumulations, they can continue to receive the benefit of interest earnings or stock appreciation on accounts associated with employment at an institution after leaving employment at that institution; this feature is commonly referred to as "portability."

## Defined Benefit Plans

In defined benefit plans the amount of the pension benefit rather than the amount of money contributed is fixed. The institution guarantees a level of pension benefits and assumes the responsibility of saving to reach that level, in some cases by requiring faculty to contribute a portion of their earnings. The institution, not the individual, makes the decisions about investing pension contributions and bears the investment risk, because it guarantees payment regardless of market performance. This can be costly: If pension fund investments do not provide enough income to cover the level of pension guaranteed, the institution must still pay the costs of the pension.

Retirees receive benefits set by a fixed formula. Formulas are typically based on a retiree's years of service at the institution, the final salary or salary averaged over several years, and a multiplication factor to convert the number of years of service and amount of salary into a pension income. Some formulas include a maximum number of years of service that can be included in the calculation.

Most defined benefit plans offered in higher education are patterned after or integrated with state employee or teacher retirement systems (Johnson, 1987:iv). Approximately 30 percent of 4-year colleges and universities, most of them public institutions, offer defined benefit plans (some also offer a defined contribution option [Daniels and Daniels, 1990a:2]). These colleges and universities employ 50 percent of all faculty at 4-year institutions. Most public 2-year colleges are also covered by defined benefit plans.

Defined benefit plans have the disadvantage of not being portable. A participant has a right to a pension that is based on a formula, not an accumulation he or she owns and keeps when moving to an institution in a different retirement system. For mobile faculty this feature can lead to a lower total pension income: A series of pensions based on short periods of service and, for the earlier jobs, lower final salaries adds up to a lower total pension income than a single pension based on the total number of years worked and the individual's final job salary (Commission on College Retirement, 1990:199, Employee Benefit Research Institute, 1990:13-14).

### Hybrid and Target Benefit Plans

A few colleges and universities limit the amount of accumulation possible in a pension fund by offering a combination of defined contribution and defined benefit plans. One university substituted a defined benefit component based on salary and years of service for the previous base contribution of 5 percent of salary to a defined contribution account and continued to match faculty contributions to the defined contribution plan up to a maximum of 5 percent of salary. The new plan provides faculty members with a larger expected pension income at age 65, but a less rapidly increasing expected income at later ages, because salary increases tend to slow or cease, and the defined benefit component rises primarily owing to the additional years of service.

A target benefit plan is a type of defined contribution plan that must meet additional IRS funding standards (Irish and Stewart, 1990; TIAA-

CREF, 1989). As in a regular defined contribution plan, the individual owns the accumulated savings and bears the investment risk. But in a target benefit plan, an employer varies its contributions to the plan on the basis of the employee's age or length of service with the aim of producing a certain level of retirement income (the "target benefit"). The target benefit is set, like the benefit in a defined benefit plan, as a function of the employee's salary, age, and years of service. The percentage of the employee's salary that the employer contributes to his or her account would vary gradually by age or years of service to produce an equal target retirement income for all employees reaching a designated normal retirement age, regardless of their years of service, or to produce a target income equal to a fixed percentage of salary times years of service.

When the estimated funds in an employee's account reach the target level, using the assumptions in the formula that determine contribution rates, the employer discontinues its contributions. The actual pension paid, however, might not equal the target amount or be equal for retirees of the same age and with the same number of years of service. As in any defined contribution plan, the amount of a pension depends on market behavior and the investment options chosen by the participant. Furthermore, a participant's expected pension income would continue to increase by the value of compounded earnings and reduced life expectancy after contributions cease. Therefore, participants still have some financial incentive to postpone retirement.

Target benefit plans are more complicated to administer than regular defined contribution plans. Unlike proposed plans in which the employer can cease contributions on the basis of estimated annuity income using past market performance (discussed below), they require the employer to make more detailed assumptions about future market performance when establishing contribution rates. In order for a target benefit plan to offer equal benefits to participants starting at different ages or equal benefits adjusted by years of service for those retiring at the same age, its contribution rates must vary by each year of age. The two or three different contribution rates currently used by institutions with defined contribution plans (with increased rates of contribution for older participants) would not achieve this goal. The IRS does not require target benefit plans to meet the same insurance and actuarial valuation requirements as defined benefit plans, but "they have somewhat more complicated annual reporting and initial determination procedures than do [defined contribution plans]" (TIAA-CREF, 1989:5).

## Incentives to Postpone Retirement

Different pension plans create different incentives for faculty who choose to postpone retirement and different costs to colleges and universities that contribute to faculty pensions. Different types of plans can also offer similar patterns of financial disincentives to retire or incentives for postponing retirement. By changing these incentives, colleges and universities may be able to change their faculty retirement patterns.

Both defined benefit and defined contribution plans (and hybrid plans) can range from inadequate to generous. In 1989 the average expenditure for pension plans at 4-year colleges and universities was 8 percent of the institution's total payroll (i.e., salary and benefits), with rates varying from less than 4 percent to more than 10 percent. Deductions from employees' pay for required pension contributions averaged 3.3 percent of payroll (TIAA-CREF, 1990). The level of the pension an employee receives depends on the formula of a defined benefit plan and on the amount contributed in a defined contribution plan. Among public institutions with defined benefit plans that set a maximum percentage of salary retirees can receive as pension income, the maximum ranges from 65 to 100 percent. The multiplication factor converting years of service and income to pension benefits ranges from 1.1 to 2.5 percent (Johnson, 1987:4-7). Institutional and faculty contributions to defined contribution plans also vary. Colleges and universities make contributions ranging from 5 percent to more than 20 percent of the salary of the individual faculty member.

Some plans, particularly those at some of the research universities at which a higher proportion of faculty now choose to remain employed up to the mandatory age, may yield retirement incomes above preretirement earnings. One such university calculated retirement incomes for a sample of 16 faculty members and found that the median proportion of preretirement salary received as pension income in the first year of retirement would be 84.5 percent if faculty retired at age 68, 95.5 percent at age 70, and 127 percent at age 75. (These calculations do not include Social Security income.) Some faculty and administrators have noted that faculty may regard pension plans generating such high retirement incomes as a source of postretirement wealth rather than of necessary personal and financial support.

Individual plans can be more generous to older faculty than to younger faculty. TIAA-CREF (1989:6) found that in 60 of its approximately 1,500 institutional plans (4 percent), the institution contributes a higher proportion of salary for older faculty members. Administrators at two such research universities say that the university instituted its policy of increasing contributions with age to encourage distinguished senior faculty to stay rather than move to other universities.

At the other end of the spectrum, both types of plans may leave faculty near retirement age with inadequate expected pension incomes despite the main features of plan design. A faculty member who has had a career at several institutions with defined benefit plans would have a pension income based on short periods of service and, for early jobs, low salaries. An individual expecting an inadequate pension as a result of mobility may postpone retirement on financial grounds. Some defined benefit plans also permit faculty to cash out the proportion of their pension funds they contributed, and some faculty in defined contribution plans have the option of cashing out all or some part of their pension accumulation when changing institutions. Faculty members who spend their pension savings when changing institutions—for example, as a means of buying a house in a more expensive community—may find pension income inadequate for retirement when they reach retirement age.

Both types of pension plans tend to reward faculty for deferring retirement. Faculty participating in either defined contribution or defined benefit pension plans can benefit substantially by remaining in employment for an additional year or more.

Pensions from defined contribution plans increase annually by the compound interest on previous accumulations, continuing personal and institutional contributions, and the inverse relationship between the level of pension payments and actuarial estimates of remaining lifespan. Table 6 shows the effects on retirement income from a defined contribution plan of 1 or 2 years additional employment. Assuming a high salary, contribution rate, and pension accumulation, we estimate that a faculty member retiring at 70 could have an expected annual pension income of approximately $60,400. If the faculty member retired instead at age 71, his or her annual pension income would be approximately $68,900; if the faculty member retired at 72, the annual pension income would be over $78,300.

If a plan does not have a maximum number of years of service that can be included in pension benefit calculations, the pension income of faculty in defined benefit plans with formulas that are based on salary and years worked increases not only with any salary increase, but also with each year worked. With an annual salary increase of 3 percent, a faculty member can increase his or her annual pension benefit by as much as 8.2 percent with an additional year of service. With an annual increase of 5 percent, an additional year's service raises pension income by as much as 10.3 percent (Rees and Smith, 1991).

The Employee Retirement Income Security Act (ERISA) reduces the financial rewards of postponing retirement beyond age 70 by requiring workers in private employment to commence drawing pension income accumulated after December 1986 no later than age 70.5. In effect, faculty reaching age 70.5 must begin paying income tax on a portion of their pension savings. Thus, faculty who continue working past age 70.5 draw both a pension and a salary. They can continue to accept pension contributions and to accrue interest on a pension account. In some cases they may be required to continue contributing to their pension funds; however, because the requirement applies annually, they must convert new accumulations to pension income by April 1 of each succeeding year. The requirement limits the financial gain possible from an additional year of employment after age 70. It also creates administrative complications for a faculty member, the institution, and the pension provider. The impact of this effect will increase over time as the number of years of earning after 1986 increases.

Many defined benefit plan formulas include a maximum number of years of service that can be used in calculating the benefit (Johnson, 1987:1-16). A faculty member reaching the maximum number of years of service can then increase pension benefits only by receiving salary increases. However, concern over possible age discrimination, ethically if not legally, has led some states that have defined benefit retirement programs to eliminate ceilings on the number of years of service included in pension calculations. A few defined benefit plan formulas set a maximum percentage of salary that an individual can receive rather than specifying a maximum number of years of service (Johnson, 1987).

Faculty in defined contribution plans benefit from continued employment through three factors that increase their pension income: compound interest on contributions, actuarial assumptions of a shortening life expectancy, and the opportunity to continue earning institutional pension contributions. Colleges and universities cannot affect the first two factors.

The status of the third factor is unclear, although it is clear that age limits are not allowed. Identical provisions in ADEA, ERISA, and the Internal Revenue Code, passed as part of the 1986 Omnibus Budget Reconciliation Act (OBRA), "require continuing contributions, allocations, and accruals in a pension plan regardless of an employee's age" (Irish and Stewart, 1990:4-5). It is unclear, however, whether years of service or total amount of contributions made can be the basis for pension contribution limits. Defined contribution plans have traditionally had no limit on the length of institutional contributions (Irish and Stewart, 1990), although under proposed IRS regulations interpreting OBRA, colleges and universities could "use non-age-based criteria to limit contributions to a defined contribution plan. For example, an employer can arguably limit the amount of benefits, years of service or years of participation" (McMorrow, 1990:33-34).

Colleges and universities lack clear legal guidelines or precedents for limiting contributions to defined contribution plans. The IRS is required to solicit comment on its proposed regulations, and the regulations are not yet in final form. Colleges and universities thus cannot be certain that in following and interpreting the proposed regulation they will meet the final requirements. They do, however, have some protection against litigation should the approved regulation differ from the proposed regulation: The preamble to the proposed regulation provides that if the final regulation does prohibit ceasing pension contributions, the rule will be applied pro-

TABLE 6   Effects on Pension Income of Working an Additional 1 or 2 Years

a. Assumptions

| | Low | Medium | High |
|---|---|---|---|
| Age 70 years and life expectancy 13.6 years | | | |
| Salary | $40,000 | $50,000 | $80,000 |
| Contribution rate | 10% | 15% | 20% |
| Annuity interest rate | 8% | 8% | 8% |
| Present value of pension account | $200,000 | $400,000 | $500,000 |
| Total annual income from pension | $24,175 | $48,346 | $60,433 |

b. Gain in account balance and pension income (based on assumptions above)

| | Working 1 Year: Age 71 Years and Life Expectancy 13 Years | | | Working Another Year: Age 72 Years and Life Expectancy 12.4 Years | | |
|---|---|---|---|---|---|---|
| | Low | Medium | High | Low | Medium | High |
| Increase in accumulation from compound interest | $16,000 | $32,000 | $40,000 | $17,280 | $34,560 | $43,200 |
| Additional contributions to pension | 4,000 | 7,500 | 16,000 | 4,000 | 7,500 | 16,000 |
| End-of-year pension account balance | 220,000 | 439,500 | 556,000 | 241,280 | 481,560 | 615,200 |
| Change in annual pension income owing to: | | | | | | |
| Change in life expectancy (-0.6) | 621 | 1,241 | 1,552 | 755 | 1,508 | 1,908 |
| Change in accumulation | 1,984 | 3,967 | 4,959 | 2,201 | 4,403 | 5,504 |
| Additional contributions | 496 | 930 | 1,984 | 496 | 930 | 1,984 |
| Total additional income from pension | 3,101 | 6,138 | 8,495 | 3,452 | 6,841 | 9,396 |
| Total annual income from pension | $27,276 | $54,484 | $68,928 | $30,727 | $61,325 | $78,323 |

*Note:* These calculations do not include adjustments for collecting pension income at age 70.5, as required by the Employee Retirement Income Security Act.

spectively only (Irish and Stewart, 1990:7). Because compound interest and actuarial reductions are the largest components of increased pension income for long-time employees in a defined contribution plan, limiting contributions would have a relatively small effect on financial incentives to continued employment (see Table 6).

Some administrators and faculty have proposed that institutions stop contributions to a defined contribution plan when a participant's annuity becomes worth enough to provide a pension income equal to some target percentage of the participant's current income—for example, 100 percent. To avoid the privacy issues inherent in determining a participant's actual pension accumulation, the college or university would estimate the worth of the annuity based on past contributions and market performance using assumptions about the participant's investment choices. This approach is cumbersome to administer and might cause the IRS to refuse to qualify the plan. Employers must meet strict nondiscrimination tests to establish whether any employee who is not highly compensated is disadvantaged by a pension plan. Employers contributing either the same percentage of compensation or dollar amount to each employee, or the same percentage or dollar amount weighted by age or years of service, qualify as nondiscriminatory under two "safe harbor" provisions. Contributing nothing to some participants' accounts on the basis of the accumulation in those accounts does not fit either safe harbor. Also, such a plan could fail the requirement that contributions be based on a definite predetermined formula, since earnings cannot be determined in advance.

## Conclusions and Recommendations

Clearly, colleges and universities have many pension plan options that they can consider. Our investigation has led us to conclude that no one pension plan design will be appropriate for all colleges and universities, and we do not endorse any particular pension plan type.

Different plan designs offer different advantages and disadvantages. For faculty, defined contribution plans, including target benefit plans, have the advantage of not penalizing mobility. However, faculty, not institutions, bear the investment risk. Defined contribution plans allow institutions to calculate pension costs with greater certainty than for other plans because costs are determined by a set rate of contributions. Target benefit plans have the disadvantage of having to satisfy more IRS requirements than do ordinary defined contribution plans, but they can save money for institutions and reduce the disincentives to retirement found in an ordinary defined contribution plan. Because institutions can limit contributions to a target benefit plan, faculty in these plans are at a somewhat greater risk of having lower pension incomes.

Defined benefit plans have different advantages and disadvantages. Institutions offering defined benefit plans face more extensive IRS requirements and bear the investment risk. If investments do not provide enough income to cover the guaranteed pension, the institution must still find funds to provide it. For faculty, defined benefit plans have the disadvantage of not being portable. The advantages and disadvantages of hybrid plans are those of their components. As discussed above, it is possible to achieve similar levels of pension income with different pension plan types. However, institutions that offer standard defined contribution plans are less able to limit inadvertent incentives to postpone retirement.

Opportunities for colleges and universities to limit pension income are restricted by the uncertain legality of capping contributions to regular defined contribution pension plans and by institutions' lack of experience with such options as target benefit plans or plans with both defined benefit and defined contribution components.

**The committee recommends that TIAA-CREF, other private pension plan providers, and state retirement systems work with institutions of higher education to develop pension plans that provide inflation-protected retirement incomes within the committee's suggested range.**

Institutions could limit their contributions to a pension plan in several ways that do not require congressional or regulatory action:

• Institutions offering defined benefit plans can limit contributions based on years of service or a maximum percentage of preretirement salary.

• Institutions offering hybrid plans, that is, contributing to both defined contribution and defined benefit plans, can limit contributions to the defined benefit component, thereby limiting overall accumulations.

• Institutions offering other kinds of plans can convert their plans to defined benefit plans or hybrid plans, although the administrative difficulties of conversion and disadvantages of defined benefit plans could outweigh the benefits.

In either case an institution can cease contributions to an existing defined contribution plan and substitute contributions to a new defined benefit or hybrid plan, but this would create administrative problems, and the institutions would have to satisfy the federal requirements regarding cessation of contributions to the old plan and the regulations governing operation of a defined benefit or hybrid plan. An institution could also convert its existing plan to a new plan type, but such a change is administratively even more difficult and expensive and is less likely to be acceptable to participants. Participants with balances that would initially purchase benefits greater than they would accrue under the new defined benefit plan formula would not accrue additional benefits. Lastly, colleges and universities choosing to offer a defined benefit pension plan or a plan with a defined benefit component would be taking on the investment risk previously borne by faculty members.

Under current federal regulations, colleges and universities that offer defined contribution plans are less able to limit the cost of their pension programs than colleges and universities offering defined benefit pension plans. Because limits to contributions disproportionately affect older faculty, it is unclear whether such limits violate age discrimination law. Although legal violations are, of course, determined by the courts, Congress and the responsible agencies could assist colleges and universities by clarifying the law and regulations governing defined contribution plans.

**The committee recommends that Congress, the Internal Revenue Service, and the Equal Employment Opportunity Commission adopt policies allowing employers to limit contributions to defined contribution plans on the basis of estimated level of pension income.**

We recognize that colleges and universities may not be able to design changes to their pension plans, negotiate the workings of proposed changes with faculty as well as pension plan providers, and put changed plans into operation by 1994 when the ADEA exemption for tenured faculty expires. Faculty would not experience the changed retirement incentives in pension plans for many years, because faculty members who are nearest retirement age own pension accumulations that are based on existing plan designs. Colleges and universities could, however, use funds saved by limiting institutional pension contributions to provide other benefits for retired faculty, such as health benefits and programs for retirees. Because health insurance benefits are less expensive when pooled, reallocation could improve the overall package of faculty retirement benefits.

### The Need for Inflation Protection and Secure Income

Approximately one-half of the defined benefit plans that are offered to faculty members include provisions for regular cost-of-living adjustments (Daniels and Daniels, 1990a:6). However, with few exceptions, these are capped at 2-5 percent annually (Johnson, 1987:10-13), with additional increases provided periodically by the state legislature. A National Bureau of Economic Research study of retirees with defined benefit plans from a range of employers found that over the period 1973-1979, the average benefit increased 24 percent while the consumer price index rose 71 percent (Munnell and Grolnic, 1986:6).

Annuities from defined contribution plans also provide imperfect inflation protection. TIAA-CREF offers a "graded payment annuity" that initially pays low benefits on the assumption that the annuity will grow to provide for future payments at a low interest rate, then increases the benefits each year based on higher actual interest rates. Nominal pension benefits rise over time to give retirees some protection against rising prices. However, graded payment annuities protect retiree incomes from inflation only to the extent that changing interest rates reflect the changing inflation rate. TIAA-CREF also offers a variable annuity based on the performance of their CREF stock portfolio, but according to Munnell and Grolnic (1986:7), "while the average return on CREF's variable annuity has been relatively high, it has also been extremely volatile; some retirees have suffered serious declines in both the real and nominal values of their retirement benefits."

One way to provide inflation protection is through indexed investments. Index bonds—that is, bonds with the coupon payment or repayment of principal indexed to some measure of inflation to guarantee a real rate of return—could provide more effective inflation protection for retirees. In other countries, notably Great Britain, the government has offered these bonds to both pension funds and individual retirees in order to provide an investment vehicle with a guaranteed rate of return. The Canadian government offers pension funds the opportunity to invest in index-linked mortgages as a vehicle for inflation-protected investment to support indexed cost-of- living adjustments (Redway, 1989).

The issuer of an index bond guarantees to pay a real rate of return by adjusting for inflation either with coupon payments or the repayment of the principal. Investors can accept a lower guaranteed real rate of return on an index bond than the expected rate of return after inflation on ordinary bonds in exchange for the lower investment risk. If the inflation adjustment is made in the coupon payments, the bond holder receives regular payments that are based on real return plus a percentage equal to average inflation over the period.

> For example, if the real rate [of return] is set at 3 percent and inflation averages 4 percent, the total annual interest cost would be 7 percent. This approach mimics the current method of compensating the lender for inflation, except that instead of trying to predict inflation at the time of the loan and incorporating this expectation into the stated nominal interest rate, actual observations on price are used to determine annual interest payments (Munnell and Grolnic, 1986:4).

This approach provides retirees with a steady real income over the period of the bond. This type of index bond, or an index bond that paid unadjusted coupon payments and repaid the principal adjusted for inflation over the period, could provide an investment vehicle that managers of defined benefit funds could use to provide pensions indexed to inflation (Munnell and Grolnic, 1986). Retirees who convert their defined contribution accumulations to an annuity could also use index bonds for more secure protection against inflation.

However, retirees and pension fund managers in this country may not have the option of indexed investments because of uncertainties about how they would be taxed. Investment and tax laws and regulations have not addressed such issues as whether nominal earnings or only real earnings would be subject to income tax. The committee is interested in the possibility of indexed investments as a way to protect faculty retirement incomes against inflation. It also recognizes that such protection could benefit all retirees. The committee believes that further study of indexed investments is needed, and it urges the IRS to examine the costs and benefits of making indexed investments available. We also encourage pension plan providers to consider them as a means of protecting pension incomes from inflation.

In the absence of indexed investments, states and colleges and universities offering defined benefit plans could reduce deterrents to retirement by providing retirees with cost-of-living adjustments that more closely reflect the inflation rate. We encourage faculty covered by defined contribution plans to take advantage of annuity payment options designed to adjust for inflation, and we encourage the organizations that administer defined contribution plans to seek better ways to protect pension incomes from inflation.

In response to calls for increased flexibility in how annuitants can collect benefits, TIAA-CREF has recently made a number of new options available, among them one that allows colleges and universities to permit their faculty to "cash out" all or a specified part of their CREF retirement funds as a lump sum drawn on retirement. (A standard TIAA-CREF annuity distribution option permits retirees to withdraw 10 percent of their accumulated funds and convert the remaining 90 percent into an annuity.) Some defined benefit plans permit a participant to collect the portion of the pension funds based on the participant's contributions. These options give a retiree the opportunity to control his or her pension accumulation, reinvesting or spending the income. However, in the context of ensuring an adequate pension income over time, allowing faculty to withdraw pension funds at or before retirement is less desirable.

Colleges and universities can allow retirees more control over the investment of their pension incomes and ensure a steady income over time by limiting complete cashouts to transfers of accumulations between providers of annuities and by limiting the amount faculty and retirees can withdraw from their pension funds as a lump sum. The committee believes the goal of providing pensions for faculty members is to ensure a continuing standard of living in retirement. It believes colleges and universities can best achieve this goal by providing payments over the course of a retirement.

## HEALTH BENEFITS

Inflation of medical care costs is running 20-22 percent annually (Johnson, 1987:31), and health insurance premiums have risen accordingly. Older faculty members and retirees report that provisions for health care, financial security, and plans for retirement are the three major factors they consider in deciding whether and when to retire (Gray, 1989; Mulanaphy, 1984). Security in retirement therefore depends not only on an adequate pension income but also on an adequate level of health coverage. There are, however, gaps in most available retiree health coverage. Institutions that offer retirees health benefits that are substantially less than employees' health benefits create a disincentive to retirement.

Faculty who consider retirement before becoming eligible for Medicare at age 65 face the prospect of purchasing medical insurance at possibly prohibitive costs unless their institution provides early retirees with health benefits. The 1985 Consolidated Omnibus Budget Reconciliation Act requires employers to offer employees who leave their employment 18 months of continued membership in a health plan, but employers can require an employee to pay the full cost of the premium, and they may also charge an additional 2 percent to cover administrative costs. A 1984 study of early retirement plans at approximately 20 institutions found that most plans did cover an early retiree's full health insurance costs until the age of normal retirement (Covert-McGrath, 1984:13). Although Medicare provides primary coverage for retirees 65 and older, it does not provide coverage as complete as most employees receive, so most retirees want secondary coverage. Some colleges and universities do provide health coverage to all retirees.

All U.S. employers and employees face the issue of rising health costs. One of our case study colleges faced a 56 percent increase in the cost of health insurance premiums in 1990. As rising medical costs have far outpaced national inflation rates, many colleges and universities have responded by contributing a lower percentage of health premiums or by reducing the amount of medical coverage they provide. In this situation colleges and universities are understandably cautious about extending health coverage to retirees (Mooney, 1988:A17): "Once established, retiree health care becomes a continuing employer obligation. In effect, health insurance has become a fully indexed benefit that is virtually an open-ended promise to cover health care for life." Chronister and Kepple (1987:43) note that an institution that extends health insurance to a retiree and hires a replacement faculty member must pay double health insurance.

Colleges and universities can compare the projected costs of offering health benefits to retirees with the costs of providing health benefits to older employees. Actuaries for one research university estimated that if the population in its employee health care plan were 1 year older, on average, the cost of the plan would be 4 percent higher. On the basis of the high proportion of faculty who retire at 70 at this university, an administrator estimated that the elimination of mandatory retirement would raise plan costs by 2.5 percent. Including retirees in a group health plan would have similar cost effects. Even if retirees pay their own premiums and thus benefit only by access to group insurance rates, their presence in the group raises the premiums paid by the institution and other participants.

Most retirement health insurance plans lack coverage for long-term care and catastrophic health care, two of the major sources of health concerns for older Americans. However, for colleges and universities, O'Brien and Woodbury (1988:11-12) note:

> . . . long-term care insurance is very expensive, perhaps as expensive as all other health benefits combined.
> Actuarial estimates vary substantially. The cost of providing the [long-term care] insurance and funding the past service liabilities for retirees, current employees, and spouses is estimated to be as much as 5 percent of payroll over 30 years.

Under most current group insurance plans for long-term care, employees pay 100 percent of the premiums, usually through payroll deductions. TIAA-CREF offers colleges and universities this type of plan. The cost to employees would be reduced if employers could pay all or part of the premium or if employees could contribute to long-term care premiums with pretax income through salary reductions under Section 125 of the Internal Revenue Code (Gajda, 1989:12).

The committee believes that concerns about health costs, like other financial concerns, should not be a deterrent to faculty retirement.

**The committee recommends that those colleges and universities that do not now provide retirees with medical coverage equal to employee coverage seek ways to improve their retirees' health care coverage by reallocating funds within the institutions' faculty compensation budgets or establishing tax-sheltered savings plans for faculty to save for their own retirement health costs.**

Colleges and universities can seek ways to improve retiree health care coverage by reallocating funds rather than increasing their total expenditures on benefits. Colleges and universities that cannot afford to provide equal health coverage for retirees and employees may nevertheless be able to reallocate funds to cover some retirement health costs. One case study public research university subsidizes retirees' annual health insurance by the dollar value of the individual's unused sick leave at retirement divided by the individual's life expectancy. Many retirees at this institution have most, if not all, of their health insurance paid by this means, although the plan is less beneficial to retirees with a history of poor health and therefore less unused sick leave.

As noted above, institutions that establish a limit to their pension contributions could allocate additional funds to retiree health benefits. This has the advantage of redirecting funds accumulated for retiree benefits to a category of retiree need. Colleges and universities with defined benefit pension funds that are larger than needed to cover retiree pensions as a result of investment performance over the past decade could use some pension funds to provide retiree health insurance. Redirected funds, however, are unlikely to cover future liabilities. The Financial Accounting Standards Board has implemented a new requirement that private sector employers providing postretirement medical benefits must accrue an expense against current income to cover the expected future costs of such benefits. Using redirected funds to cover only current retiree health costs leaves the question of future provision unresolved.

Colleges and universities unable to fund additional medical benefits for faculty should explore ways to assist faculty in saving for health and long-term care insurance in retirement by organizing tax-sheltered savings plans. Since Medicare is the primary provider for retirees over 65, retired faculty over 65 need only supplemental coverage in order to have total coverage equal to preretirement coverage.

Offering tax-deferred savings for retirement health costs, like changing pension plans, is unlikely to have an immediate effect on faculty retirement decisions, since older faculty will have less time to accumulate savings before retirement. Colleges and universities could, however, make retirement a more attractive option by reallocating their faculty benefit budgets to provide better retiree health benefits.

The health care cost crisis cannot be resolved entirely within the framework of higher education. The rising cost of medical care creates financial concerns not only for faculty, retired faculty, and institutions of higher education but for people and institutions in all sectors of the economy. Faculty, administrators, and state higher education boards should be active participants in what must be a nationwide discussion and national policy making.

## CONTINUED FACULTY PERQUISITES FOR RETIREES

Many faculty members who are facing retirement are concerned about continuing access to academic life, including opportunities for professional pursuits, office space, clerical support, parking privileges, and other faculty perquisites. In the words of one university task force report sent to the committee:

> The change to retirement can be enriching and stimulating, but it often is accompanied with fears regarding the loss of identity and purpose. The task force feels that a number of steps can be taken by the University to improve the status and welfare of the emeritus professors. Invitations to

colloquia, the continuation of parking and library privileges, the opportunity to teach an occasional course, access to an office, inclusion in departmental social activities, and the opportunity to be undergraduate advisors, all can contribute to the self esteem of retired professors and can add enormously to the intellectual resources of the University.

Studies (e.g., Daniels and Daniels, 1990b:75) show that faculty members who are considering retirement are concerned about maintaining some contact with students and colleagues and carrying on research and other professional activity. Rowe found that 40 percent of the retired academics in his study were reemployed, most in teaching or research (cited in Patton, 1979:57). Kellams and Chronister (1988:12) found that 81 percent of retirees listed academic and professional activities among their postretirement activities. They also report "a large number of retirees pursuing academic/professional activities were doing so without remuneration" (Kellams and Chronister, 1988:15).

A faculty member whose desire to postpone retirement is not based on financial need may find continued perquisites an attractive retirement incentive. For example, a researcher eligible for full pension benefits may be unwilling to give up access to a laboratory. A teacher ready to slow down may appreciate some advising duties as a way to maintain contact with students. The range of possible perquisites include: office space, library access, administrative support, and computer use; laboratory space and access; inclusion on departmental and institutional mailing lists and invitations to events; participation in departmental administration; retention of principal investigator status; bookstore discounts; faculty club membership; reduced tuition for family members; and even programs that provide retired faculty with temporary or permanent employment. Unlike phased and partial retirement programs, such programs may or may not be academic posts: Felicetti (1982) suggests universities facilitate consulting opportunities for retired faculty by making a brochure for local business contacts or putting older faculty in touch with organizations like the Service Corps of Retired Executives. The California Conference of the American Association of University Professors (AAUP) has listed 39 such benefits in its "Bill of Rights for Emeriti" (Albert, 1986).

At one of our case study uncapped public research universities, the estimated costs of providing an active retiree with a 100-square-foot office; free parking; an average of 3 hours of secretarial assistance weekly; $25 in office supplies, photocopying, and postage monthly; and the telephone, library, and computer access provided to regular faculty would total $4,124 annually. The marginal cost of these perquisites can be prohibitive at colleges and universities at which space or services are scarce, costly, or fully utilized. For example, one of our case study urban universities cannot provide parking for all its current faculty and so regards parking for retirees as impossible. Lab space and equipment are costly for all colleges and universities.

Colleges and universities seldom calculate the costs of providing retiree benefits (Chronister, 1990; COFHE, 1989; Mauch, 1990). One reason these institutions may be unable to do so is that many perquisites are handled informally on a departmental basis. Benefits for retired faculty tend to depend on tradition and precedent rather than written policies, with decisions about what to allocate to each retiree made on an ad hoc basis (COFHE, 1989; Mauch, 1990). Like ad hoc retirement incentives, this approach has the advantage of flexibility and the disadvantages of potential inequity and uncertainty. Comments from retired faculty during our case study visits suggest that they appreciate formal benefits: One retiree noted that "it's good not to have to rely on being a friend of the dean." Yet faculty also value the opportunity to maintain connections with their department as well as with the university. Retirees and administrators at several of our case study institutions indicated that retirees generally preferred office space in their department to space in areas set aside for retiree offices.

At two case study universities that have emeriti centers, retired faculty are organized into an active and activist presence on campus, volunteering in campus activities and special events, attending and offering courses, assisting with retirement counseling, and acting as advocates for older people's interests. The centers are funded by a combination of membership dues and institutional funds.

**Colleges and universities can ease the transition from employment to retirement for faculty by providing ways for retirees to continue relations with the institution.** The benefits offered can vary based on what the institution can afford to provide and the interests of its retired faculty. They need not be part of a formal phased retirement incentive program (discussed in Chapter 5).

We believe both retirees and institutions can benefit from continued relations. We therefore encourage colleges and universities that do not already give retired faculty library privileges, list them in directories, keep them on mailing lists, and invite them to occasions such as commencements and receptions to do so. The committee also encourages departments to consider finding ways for retired faculty members to continue to contribute—for example, by sitting on dissertation committees, acting as informal advisers to students or less experienced colleagues, offering lectures or an occasional course, or continuing some research. Allocating scarcer and more expensive benefits such as office and laboratory space will be more difficult. In the likely event that demand for some perquisites will exceed supply, we recommend that colleges and universities develop procedures for allocating these resources. We suggest that, if they are permitted to do so, colleges and universities offer these opportunities to retirees on a renewable merit basis—for example, 1 year at a time with renewals at the discretion of the department or institution. This approach would allow the department or institution to reallocate scarce resources on the basis of continuing merit, scholarly or teaching contributions, grant or contract renewals, and competing needs.

Some universities who estimate that a large proportion of their faculty would postpone retirement beyond age 70 if allowed to do so base those projections partly on the number of retirees over age 70 who maintain an active connection with the university. In many cases departments already provide some office space and arrange for retirees to teach courses or continue research projects. Although older faculty may prefer full faculty privileges to the perquisites available to retirees, they may be willing to accept reduced privileges in exchange for the reduced responsibilities and greater freedom of retirement. When access to colleagues, students, or institutional facilities, rather than financial concerns, leads faculty to postpone retirement, providing continued faculty perquisites to retirees could lead to more retirements and free up institutional resources and faculty positions.

## RETIREMENT PLANNING

A quote from one faculty report on changing retirement policies captures the goal of retirement planning for colleges, universities, and individual faculty members (Holland, 1988:12): "The objective should be to convert retirement from what is an undesired (and virtually unforeseen) catastrophe, to a more meaningful and acceptable stage of academic life." To the extent that retirement planning assistance makes retirement a familiar and normal career prospect, colleges and universities can make retirement a more attractive option for faculty. Increased faculty options, ranging from the opportunity to continue working beyond age 70 to choices resulting from retirement incentives or changed retirement policies, may make individual planning more difficult and increase faculty members' needs for formalized planning assistance and retirement counseling.

TIAA-CREF surveys have found a positive correlation between faculty retirees who reported satisfaction with retirement and those who reported they spent time planning for financial security and substantive activities in retirement. This correlation could be due to self-selection, if faculty who already regard retirement positively are more likely to plan for it. Nevertheless, evidence from our case study visits suggests that the availability of competent and personalized planning assistance can relieve faculty worries about retirement. The benefits offices at two public research universities, one uncapped and one capped, offer regular seminars on retirement and financial planning; the latter seminars include a component on pensions as a way of providing retirement information to younger as well as older faculty.

Benefits office staff also provide faculty with individual retirement counseling, opportunities to talk to retired colleagues, and help in coordinating the paperwork associated with retirement.

Some smaller institutions also provide planning assistance. At one case study liberal arts college, the dean discusses career goals, which can include plans for retirement, with all faculty members. The college has used part of a grant from a private foundation to fund outside financial consultants for faculty members who mention an interest in financial planning for retirement; administrators decided that outside consultants would be independent of institutional bias. Faculty members are free to choose any consultant, although the dean will provide a list of reputable firms that have been used in the past.

One private research university task force recommended that the university provide a financial incentive to encourage faculty to plan for retirement. It recommended that the university contribute to financial planning twice in the career of all long-term employees, and it proposed a salary bonus equal to one-half of a year's salary to any faculty member between ages 59 and 67 who declared retirement plans 3-5 years in advance. The task force concluded this bonus "is sufficiently large to cause faculty to think about their retirement plans."

Colleges and universities as well as individual faculty members benefit from coordinated and visible retirement planning programs: Faculty members are more likely to plan for retirement when they receive assistance, and colleges and universities that help faculty plan for retirement have an opportunity to monitor retirement concerns. They can use the resulting awareness of retirement plans and needs to improve both retirement programs and projections of faculty supply and demand.

**The committee recommends that, in order to make retirement a more familiar and normal career prospect, all colleges and universities assist their faculty in planning for retirement.**

Since some retirement concerns have to do with specific institutional retirement policies and benefits, adequate retirement planning assistance requires more than an annual visit from a pension plan representative. At a few case study institutions, a dean or a retirement planning coordinator works with retirement plan providers to ensure that faculty know about their retirement options throughout their careers; faculty are able to consider retirement options in the context of their individual needs; and faculty are able to benefit from others' experience with retirement. But at most of our case study colleges and universities, there is no one person or office to contact for information on retirement; at some, faculty do not even know which offices handle retirements and retiree benefits.

Retirement planning could supplement each of the policy changes discussed in this chapter. Additional financial information assists faculty in determining the adequacy of their pension incomes and other retirement benefits, including health benefits and income from retirement incentive programs. Nonfinancial counseling can increase faculty awareness of retirement options, including programs and perquisites for retirees. Retirement counseling can also assist colleges and universities in developing retirement policies. Both financial and nonfinancial planning assistance may make retirement more attractive by making it less of an unknown state.

**Retirement benefit policies—pension plans, health benefits and continued faculty perquisites for retirees, and retirement planning assistance—can affect faculty retirement decisions.** Colleges and universities may be able to increase faculty turnover by changing these policies. Faculty and administrators can also consider changes in these policies to address institutional concerns about increasing costs and individual concerns about retirement security. Colleges and universities seeking ways to increase faculty turnover, including those that may suffer reduced turnover if mandatory retirement is eliminated, may also want to consider policies specifically designed to encourage faculty retirements. We address retirement incentive programs in the next chapter.

# 5

# Retirement Incentive Programs

Retirement incentive programs, unlike retirement benefit programs (discussed in Chapter 4), are specifically designed to encourage faculty turnover, typically by offering part-time employment or payment in exchange for an agreement to retire. Over the past decade some colleges and universities have offered retirement incentive programs to faculty in response to the 1977-1982 change in the mandatory retirement age from 65 to 70, when states eliminated mandatory retirement, and in some cases in anticipation of the possible nationwide end of mandatory retirement. Colleges and universities instituted these plans to deal with faculty turnover issues specific to the campus, the state higher education system, or all public employees.

Both colleges and universities and faculty members can benefit from retirement incentives programs. Colleges and universities can offer these programs to increase faculty turnover in specific areas for a limited time. Faculty members can accept retirement incentive programs as a means of making up for fewer years of accumulating pension benefits and of making a gradual transition to retirement.

Colleges and universities that consider offering retirement incentives face several issues: which type of program will be attractive to faculty not otherwise planning to retire, what will be the cost of offering a program, what will be the legality of different program designs, and whether to restrict incentives to particular individuals or groups of faculty. In this chapter the committee considers these issues, particularly in light of the possible elimination of mandatory retirement.

## TYPES OF FORMAL PROGRAMS

The Commission on College Retirement estimated that in 1985 25-30 percent of American colleges and universities had begun offering a wide range of retirement incentive programs designed to encourage faculty to set a retirement date in exchange for a reduced teaching load, retirement incentives, or both (Watkins, 1985:21). According to our case studies and letters from faculty and administrators, and the literature on retirement incentive programs for faculty, the characteristics of the programs vary:

• Most plans require a minimum number of years of service for eligibility; that number ranges from 10 to 20 years, usually including time spent on sabbaticals but not leave without pay (Covert-McGrath, 1984).

• Most plans are open only to tenured faculty.

• For plans that limit faculty participation on the basis of age, the ages of eligibility vary: for example, 50-65, 55-70.

• Many programs require faculty to set a specific retirement date. Some programs require faculty to apply 90 days to 1 year before their desired retirement date, but others require as much as 4-10 years notice.

• Most plans cover full health benefits until retirees reach age 65 (i.e., the age of eligibility for Medicare).

• Common additional benefits offered include disability benefits, medical plan membership, tuition benefits for the retiree and his or her dependents, free admission to campus activities, a one-time lump sum payment in addition to severance pay, and preretirement planning assistance.

More broadly, retirement incentive programs can be differentiated by whether they offer part-time employment or require full retirement. Two types of programs offer faculty the opportunity to work part time before fully retiring (see Chronister and Clevenger, 1986a):

1. In partial retirement programs faculty members draw pension benefits while returning to work part time.

2. In phased retirement programs retirement plan contributions continue during the period of part-time employment, and program participants draw their retirement benefits only after full retirement.

For example, a college or university could allow its tenured faculty to work half time at half salary in exchange for an agreement to fully retire at the end of 3 years. Retirees in a partial retirement program can use the income from part-time employment to supplement pension payments that have been reduced by fewer years of pension accumulation and a longer life expectancy. Retirees in a phased retirement program do not draw their pension income and have only part-time earnings during the phased retirement period. Colleges and universities can supplement the part-time income with supplemental annuities or lump-sum payments.

In some programs the institution guarantees that participants can continue to work as long as they wish, provided that they notify the administration each year of their intentions to work part time for an additional year.

In other programs participants agree to full retirement after a fixed number of years of part-time work. Some programs at colleges and universities with a mandatory retirement age permit faculty to work part time until they reach the mandatory retirement age. By offering a program that includes a fixed retirement date, colleges and universities decrease uncertainty about when faculty intend to retire. Our case studies of institutions with programs that do not limit the number of years of reemployment suggest that partly retired faculty find retirement attractive: Most faculty who work part time choose to retire completely after 2 or 3 years (see also Chronister and Clevenger, 1986a).

Trial retirement is another alternative to full retirement. Colleges and universities can permit faculty members to return to full-time employment after a trial period of retirement or apply lenient leave-of-absence policies to faculty members who are considering retirement. Some colleges and universities allow a semester's or year's leave of absence with full or half pay, or leave without pay, to faculty who are unsure about whether they are ready to retire (Spreadbury, 1984:16). Like phased and partial retirement programs, trial retirement allows faculty to cut back professional commitments without completely giving up employment.

The opportunity to try retirement without relinquishing one's job can be a retirement incentive for faculty who are already eligible for a full pension or would be eligible after the period of leave. Trial retirees may find they like retirement and choose not to return. One of our case study institutions reported that few faculty who took trial retirement subsequently returned to employment.

Full retirement incentive programs offer a range of benefits in exchange for an agreement to retire. Most programs include financial benefits, such as

* lump-sum severance payments or additional credit in a defined benefit pension plan, offered at a flat rate or on the basis of age, salary, length of service, or some combination of these;
* annual payments from the institutional budget equal to full preretirement salary or a percentage of it, which can be based on age, salary, or service; and
* institutional purchases of supplemental annuities.

These financial benefits can provide retirees with the additional income needed for a longer period of retirement and make up for earlier than anticipated end of contributions to the regular pension plan. From a faculty member's perspective, incentives to full retirement can make earlier retirement financially possible.

Chronister and Trainer (1985:193) describe "bridging programs," which offer retirees an income to bridge the gap between the last year of employment and the first year of eligibility for full retirement benefits. This permits retirees to put off collecting their regular retirement annuity rather than trying to make the accumulation in a defined contribution program last for a longer number of years.

Some colleges and universities provide additional benefits as part of retirement incentive programs. Covert-McGrath (1984:15) found that some colleges and universities paid for or subsidized retirees' medical benefits and life insurance coverage. In most cases these benefits ceased at age 65, when retirees became eligible for Medicare, or at the mandatory retirement age.

## COSTS AND BENEFITS OF FORMAL PROGRAMS

Retirement incentive programs may not save money if some participating faculty members might have retired anyway at no additional cost to the institution. For example, a program could provide a faculty member who had always intended to retire at 62 with a financial bonus for doing so. Administrators can compare the cost of incentive payments to the salaries and benefits program that participants would have received had they not retired, but there is no clear way to estimate when participating faculty would have chosen to retire in the absence of an incentive. Our case studies and discussions with benefits and finance administrators suggest that at least some colleges and universities are modifying or cutting back retirement incentive programs that proved more costly or less successful than expected. However, other colleges and universities have found budget-neutral ways to offer retirement incentive programs—for example, by spending funds from an overfunded defined benefit pension plan on financial incentives to retirement.

The Consortium on Financing Higher Education found, in a 1987 survey of its member colleges and universities and a set of public universities, that the reported savings or costs of retirement incentive programs ranged from $2 million saved from eight retirements to programs designed to break even and to estimated costs of $60,000-$500,000 per year. One college commented that "the staffing flexibility feature far outweighed the additional expense" (Consortium on Financing Higher Education, 1987:46-52).

Surveys have shown not only that many faculty like the idea of part-time retirement but also that phased and partial retirement programs are the only incentive programs that appeal to faculty who report they are not planning to retire in the near future (Carlson, 1990:35; Patton, 1979). Consequently, plans involving part-time employment may be more likely than other retirement incentives to encourage faculty to retire sooner than they otherwise would have.

These options have the potential to benefit the institution by continuing to utilize the talents of senior faculty and permitting the institution to plan effectively [for faculty retirements]. They have the potential to benefit faculty by providing mental stimulation, the opportunity to continue to interact with colleagues and students and a financial and psychological transition into full retirement (Daniels and Daniels, 1989:38).

Phased and partial programs can provide financial benefits for both faculty members and institutions. At one institution faculty in the partial retirement program receive a pension equal to approximately one-half of their preretirement salary in addition to earning 40 percent of their preretirement salary for part-time employment. When this income is supplemented by Social Security and any tax benefits resulting from a lower taxable income, some retirees earn more than they did when fully employed. Moreover, the institution saves 60 percent of the faculty member's salary (Chronister and Clevenger, 1986b). Some colleges and universities use such savings to hire new faculty at lower salaries. The cost of supporting a partial retiree varies depending on whether the partial retiree needs an office, secretarial services, and other perquisites for part of a year or year round. The savings from a partial retirement may not always be enough to fund hiring a replacement for the retiree.

Colleges and universities can offer incentives to full retirement in the form of severance payments, supplemental annuities, or any payment in exchange for an agreement to retire. Some colleges and universities offer additional salary or pension benefits to faculty members who agree to retire in a specified number of years. For example, a faculty member agreeing to retire in 5 years could receive a bonus payment or 5 years of additional service credit in a defined benefit pension plan.

Poorly constructed programs, however, can result in costly and inefficient strategies, such as paying 2 years' worth of salary as a retirement incentive to faculty members who had already intended to retire in 2 years or less or encouraging more faculty members to retire than the institution is able to replace. Patton (1979:187) found that the offer of a payment equal to 1-2 years' salary in exchange for agreement to retire appealed to a large number of employees, but primarily to those who reported that they intended to retire within 1 or 2 years.

The 1986 Tax Reform Act complicated financial incentives to full retirement by requiring employees to pay taxes on severance pay or the amount of a supplemental annuity in the year of retirement rather than spreading the payments over the course of retirement as the income is received. Colleges and universities may need to cover part or all of the additional tax cost in order to make full-time early retirement attractive under the new regulations. Two universities calculated this would cost approximately 20 percent of the original bonus figure. One case study uncapped public research university ameliorates tax disincentives by paying a lump-sum incentive in two installments spread over the academic year so as to fall into two tax years, with the amount of the second installment (paid in the first full year of retirement) set below the maximum outside income permitted for full Social Security benefits.

Some administrators fear that offering a retirement incentive may lead productive faculty to choose early retirement while unproductive faculty or faculty in overstaffed departments do not retire. Faculty who are considering positions elsewhere might accept an offer of a supplemental annuity or lump-sum payment that is too small to make up for lost pension or salary income, while employees actually planning to retire would find such an offer less attractive (Patton, 1979:192).

In a review of discrimination law related to retirement incentives, McMorrow (1990:19) concludes that a plan may offer retirement incentives to only a subset of an institution's employees as long as nondiscriminatory factors explain the exclusion.

There are at least four ways that current retirement incentive plans limit participation. First, programs may target specific departments. One university calculated overstaffing in its departments and gave members of the most overstaffed departments priority in participating in a retirement incentive program (Chronister and Clevenger, 1986:29).

Second, incentives are based on salary. A lump-sum payment based on the mean salary of all faculty offers, in effect, a greater proportion of income to low earners than to high earners. Stanford University offered a program that linked the level of the incentive payment an individual would receive to the median departmental salary "on the assumption that salary level is an indication of quality" (Chronister and Kepple, 1987:31).

Third, some institutions retain the right to deny participation to individuals or to delay their participation. One university reserves the right to delay its acceptance of a faculty member's statement of intent to participate in the early retirement program by up to 12 months. It exercises this right when unable to find a replacement for the early retiree (Chronister and Clevenger, 1986a:12). One of our case study uncapped public universities retains the right to reject some faculty who apply for its incentive program in order to keep program costs at or below a statutory percentage of its personnel budget. Selection is based on a formula using age (for cost-justified reasons), years of service, salary history (positive for those receiving lower raises), and an additional optional factor to account for "management needs."

Fourth, institutions limit participation based on age. The 1990 Older Workers Benefit Protection Act made it clearly legal to set a minimum age for participation in retirement incentive programs. It also made it clearly legal to provide "bridge" payments until retirees are eligible for Social Security, effectively limiting an incentive to employees under age 65. One of our case study public universities set a maximum age for participation in its retirement incentive program after initially opening the program to all employees under a grandfather clause. The university developed this program in consultation with the state attorney general (although in recent legislation Congress did not clarify the legal status of upper age limits for participation).

Colleges and universities can avoid offering retirement incentives to faculty more likely to retire anyway by offering plans that provide younger employees with benefits equal to those received by older employees (McMorrow, 1990). For example, colleges and universities with defined benefit plans can offer retirees over age 60 benefits equal to those they would have received at age 65, rather than making the usual actuarial reduction of their pension income. Such an offer gives nothing extra to employees already aged 65 or older. As noted above, the legal status of offering younger employees benefits that are denied to older employees is less clear.

Colleges and universities that offer retirement incentive programs must be careful to ensure that their programs are legal. Under ADEA, an employer found guilty of age discrimination is liable for damages equal to double the affected employees' lost wages if the court finds the violation of ADEA "willful"—that is, showing "reckless disregard for the legality of its acts" (McMorrow, 1990:3-4). Courts have rejected plans when they found provisions too complicated for participants to understand, when employers failed to give employees sufficient time to consider the offer, and when employees were pressed into decisions (McMorrow, 1990:43-44).

Administrators can change or withdraw retirement incentive programs that are not offered as employee benefit programs. Colleges and universities can distinguish a program from ongoing employee benefit programs by offering it for a limited time period or to a limited number of employees. Colleges and universities have offered retirement incentive programs limited to periods ranging from 1 month to 1 year. For example, one college "established a five month window during which faculty could contract for an immediate or deferred early retirement" in exchange for severance payments based on age at retirement (Chronister and Clevenger 1986b:8).

Legal guidelines are unclear for programs not classified as employee benefit plans. Some administrators are concerned that any ongoing retirement incentive program may be classified as an employee benefit and therefore as an expensive liability under ERISA funding requirements. Classification of retirement incentive programs as employment benefits also raises legal questions of discrimination regarding whether colleges and universities have to extend the program to nonfaculty employees. In some cases colleges and universities are considering whether to discontinue programs that they cannot afford either to fund as faculty benefits or to extend.

State laws also affect plan design. For example, some states (e.g., Washington) forbid public institutions to pay people for services not rendered, thereby ruling out the use of state funds for severance payments, although phased and partial retirement programs are permitted. Other states (e.g., Ohio) prevent public employers from guaranteeing reemployment (including part-time employment) to retirees: Any partial employment after a retiree begins drawing pension benefits must be arranged after retirement, so faculty members must agree to retire full time and gamble on being reemployed (Chronister and Kepple, 1987:49). Some public institutions have had difficulties with state retirement incentive programs designed for all state employees. At one public case study university, faculty who wanted to accept a state retirement incentive were required to make their retirement decisions over the summer, after teaching assignments had been arranged, and to retire by a date in the middle of the semester. The university then had to scramble to adjust course offerings and faculty assignments.

**The committee recommends that states offering retirement incentive programs to all state employees consider the impact of the program on state institutions of higher education and consider program designs or exceptions in program rules to avoid disrupting state colleges and universities.**

## INDIVIDUAL BUYOUTS

Colleges and universities have traditionally arranged retirement incentives for individual faculty members on an ad hoc basis when the goal was to retire a specific individual. This method enables colleges and universities to obtain a desired retirement without any risk of the incentive attracting more productive individuals. It also allows the selected faculty member to negotiate an incentive tailored to his or her individual needs, such as health insurance benefits, a lump-sum payment, or continued university housing (Chronister and Kepple, 1987). However, individually tailored offers can be less beneficial to faculty: Offers limited to selected employees can favor those in a better bargaining position or those who are simply more adept at bargaining.

The variable nature of both the benefits and the selection of participants can lead to legal problems for colleges and universities. If the criteria are informal, an institution has less defense against a charge of discrimination. In particular, participation in programs must be voluntary to be legal, and targeted individual buyouts may not meet this criterion if the first approach is made by the institution to the individual rather than vice versa (Chronister and Kepple, 1987; McMorrow, 1990:45-46). Colleges and universities that offer individual retirement incentives can lessen the risk of a lawsuit by making the offer a matter of individual choice; by allowing the potential retiree time to consider the offer, as with formal retirement incentive programs; and possibly by asking individuals to waive their right to a legal challenge of the agreement. Waivers have the advantage of putting the "employee on notice of the existence of federal and state age discrimination law, indicating that the employee is making a knowledgeable decision" (McMorrow, 1990:46-55).

Individual buyouts could create perverse incentives for nonperforming faculty to stay on in hopes of being bought out. This has harmed the collegial atmosphere at some colleges and universities. The University of Minnesota Mandatory Retirement Task Force (1989:7) states:

> If the case is one in which discharge is appropriate, the use of major economic resources to save the unit head from the turmoil of discharge proceedings may not be justified. Furthermore, productive members of the department are outraged by the use of large resources in problem cases; the message delivered is that to get these resources you need to become a problem case.

Individual buyouts are most appropriate when used with sensitivity to faculty members' sense of equity. When faculty members voluntarily agree to the incentives offered, individual buyouts can be an effective way of encouraging faculty to retire.

## CONCLUSIONS AND RECOMMENDATIONS

Retirement incentive programs, which have been widely used in higher education, can significantly affect faculty retirement behavior. Colleges and universities can offer retirement incentive programs for fields or department in which turnover is most needed and can limit participation to control both turnover and costs. Because acceptance of a retirement incentive must be voluntary, these programs create additional retirement options for faculty—not forced retirements. These programs can offer faculty financial benefits and the opportunity to make a gradual transition to retirement. Whether these plans are money savers for the institution or are a way of exchanging a retirement problem for a financial one will vary with the circumstances of the institution. **The committee concludes that retirement incentive programs are clearly an important tool for increasing turnover and one that must be considered by any college or university concerned about the effects of retirement.**

The committee emphasizes that retirement incentive programs and individual retirement incentive contracts must be entered into freely and without coercion, when seen by both the institution and the individual as beneficial. Although it is unlikely that colleges and universities would tie a retirement agreement to the granting of tenure, in order to avoid the possibility of coercion, we believe colleges and universities should limit offers of retirement incentive programs or individualized retirement incentives to tenured faculty. It is inappropriate to offer retirement incentives to faculty being considered for tenure.

**The committee recommends that states and colleges and universities that offer retirement incentives to all employees develop ways to protect faculty who are being considered for tenure from possible coercion.**

It is also inappropriate to ask a faculty member to decide whether a retirement incentive offer would be beneficial when retirement is only a remote prospect.

**The committee recommends that colleges and universities offer retirement incentive programs and individual retirement incentive contracts only to faculty who are ready to consider seriously when to retire.**

Retirement incentive programs now used in higher education are commonly designed for faculty in their 60s. By extending participation in retirement incentive programs to faculty aged 50 or over, colleges and universities could benefit by increasing faculty turnover and in planning for faculty retirements. We believe 50 would be an appropriate minimum age.

**The committee recommends that colleges and universities offer retirement incentive programs and individual retirement incentive contracts only to tenured faculty age 50 and over.**

In the 1990 Older Workers Benefit Protection Act, which extended employee protection against age discrimination, Congress clearly permitted retirement incentive programs that include a minimum age for participation, are offered for a window of time, and provide bridge payments made until retirees are eligible for Social Security. However, the legal status of some features of retirement incentive programs may still need clarification; Congress and the responsible federal agencies could assist colleges and universities by clearly preserving several options.

**The committee recommends that Congress, the Internal Revenue Service, and the Equal Employment Opportunity Commission permit colleges and universities to offer faculty voluntary retirement incentive programs that: are not classified as an employee benefit, include an upper age limit for participants, and limit participation on the basis of institutional needs.**

Retirement incentive programs give colleges and universities the opportunity to offer a policy aimed directly at changing a particular aspect of faculty retirement behavior. For example, colleges and universities concerned about decreased turnover during a transition period following the elimination of mandatory retirement could offer retirement incentive programs limited to the projected transition period. Colleges and universities wanting to increase turnover in a particular school or department could give the faculty in that school or department priority in accepting incentives.

However, colleges and universities that are considering retirement incentive programs need to plan carefully to design a program that is appropriate to faculty and institutional needs, including the needs to support new fields, allocate resources wisely, and respond to faculty concerns about retirement. Congress could assist colleges and universities in this effort by ensuring that a wide range of options is available.

# 6

# Conclusions and Recommendations

Congress asked the committee "to analyze the potential consequences of the elimination of mandatory retirement in institutions of higher education" (Age Discrimination Employment Act [ADEA], 1986, Section 12(c)). In this chapter we present the conclusions and recommendations we have reached on the basis of our research (discussed in preceding chapters) and the committee members' extensive experience as faculty, administrators, and trustees at a range of colleges and universities.

## EFFECTS OF ELIMINATING MANDATORY RETIREMENT

### Two Key Conclusions

**At most colleges and universities few tenured faculty would continue working past age 70 if mandatory retirement is eliminated.**

Most faculty retire before age 70. At many colleges and universities the average faculty retirement age is below 65. Furthermore, patterns of faculty retirement have remained stable over time, even though the mandatory retirement age has been raised from 65 to 70 and, at some institutions, has been eliminated. The proportion of faculty over age 65 is now low, and it has been low over the past decade. All of the uncapped colleges and universities with data report that the proportion of faculty over age 70 is less than 1.6 percent.

**At some research universities a high proportion of faculty would choose to work past age 70 if mandatory retirement is eliminated.**

Faculty at research universities retire later on average than faculty at other institutions. At a small number of research universities, more than 40

103

percent of the faculty who retire each year have done so at the current mandatory retirement age of 70. (At most other institutions few or no faculty members work until age 70.) Evidence suggests that faculty members who are actively engaged in research are more likely than others to work past age 65. More generally, faculty who are research oriented, enjoy inspiring students, have light teaching loads, and are covered by pension plans that reward later retirement are more likely to work past age 70. These factors are not unique to research universities, but they are present to a greater degree at some of those institutions than at other types of colleges and universities.

## Consequences for Institutions and Faculty

**If mandatory retirement is eliminated, some research universities are likely to suffer adverse effects from low faculty turnover: increased costs and limited flexibility to respond to changing needs and to support new fields by hiring new faculty.**

The committee notes that new fields of scholarship are a source of vitality for research and teaching and that colleges and universities enter new fields and expand their coverage of fields by hiring new faculty. Research universities at which a significant number of faculty work past age 70 would have fewer available positions and thus would be less able to hire either prospective junior faculty or more senior faculty from other institutions, which would limit their ability to enter new fields. This loss of flexibility would also limit opportunities for some prospective faculty who would otherwise have been offered positions at those research universities. However, faculty qualified for positions at adversely affected research universities are likely to attract offers from other research universities.

Postponed retirements will increase costs at those research universities—and any other colleges and universities—at which a significant number of faculty work past age 70. If an institution expands its faculty as a way of supporting new fields, costs will increase. Our modeling exercise (see Chapter 2) suggests that faculty salary budgets could increase by 1-2 percent over the first 5 years and another 1-2 percent over the following 10 years. Costs would rise even without additional hiring as the average age of faculty members rises, because, on average, salaries and benefits increase with age.

**Administrators and faculty can best assess the potential impact of uncapping at their own colleges and universities by studying their faculty age distributions, retirement patterns, and hiring needs.**

The effects of uncapping on any college or university depend on its proportion of older faculty, on whether the faculty choose to work past age

70, and on whether the institution plans to expand or reduce its faculty size. The committee believes the impact will be small at most colleges and universities.

In sum, the elimination of mandatory retirement could limit hiring flexibility and adversely affect some institutions, particularly some research universities. The committee believes that Congress and institutions of higher education need to seek nondiscriminatory ways to avoid those adverse effects.

A faculty member's retirement decision is a complex one that depends on individual factors—such as continuing career interests, health, and personal finances—as well as on incentives, intentional and unintentional, in an institution's retirement policies. No one policy lever can create faculty turnover or reduce costs at all institutions or under all circumstances. Therefore, we have considered a number of options that colleges and universities could use to increase their ability to hire and to maintain their quality (Chapters 3, 4, and 5). Since individual retirement decisions can involve a number of factors, we have also considered ways that Congress, regulatory agencies, and state legislatures and agencies could help colleges and universities avoid the adverse effects of eliminating mandatory retirement (Chapters 4 and 5).

**An increase in the number of faculty over age 70 or, more generally, an increase in the average age of faculty does not necessarily affect institutional quality.**

Although there is little evidence on age and research quality, the evidence on age and cognitive abilities, age and teaching, and age and rates of publication suggests that faculty in their 70s can continue to perform well and that there are variations in performance among faculty of any age. However, in some cases a faculty member may fall into patterns of poor teaching and uninspired research. The committee believes many of these cases have been mistakenly attributed to inevitable age-related declines. Available evidence does not show significant declines caused by age.

**Eliminating mandatory retirement would not pose a threat to tenure.**

Tenure is intended to protect academic freedom, not to protect faculty against dismissal for inadequate performance. Tenure affords a guarantee of due process. Colleges and universities can dismiss tenured faculty provided they afford due process in a clearly defined and understood dismissal procedure in which the institution bears the burden of proof, although dismissal of faculty members for poor performance is rare now and likely to remain rare. There is no evidence that the number of inadequate faculty would increase if faculty were allowed to work past age 70; some evidence suggests that poor performers may be less likely to keep working past age 65.

Faculty performance evaluation can be a useful tool for maintaining and improving faculty quality, particularly when administrators and faculty use it to provide faculty with feedback on the quality of their work and on how their activities fit disciplinary and institutional directions. Most colleges and universities already use reviews by colleagues and administrators to assess faculty performance, usually as part of such actions as promotions and sometimes as part of allocating resources such as salary increases, internal grant funds, and sabbaticals.

**The committee recommends that faculty and administrators work to develop ways to provide faculty with feedback on their performance.**

The committee believes faculty and administrators can find collegial, informal, and positive ways to assist some faculty who get stuck in unproductive scholarship or teaching. However, there is evidence that elaborate systems for review may not be worth the additional effort and cost. Colleges and universities hoping to hire scholars in new fields or to change the balance of faculty research and teaching interests will need to encourage turnover using mechanisms other than performance evaluation and dismissal.

## RETIREMENT POLICIES

### Retirement Incentive Programs

**Retirement incentive programs are clearly an important tool for increasing turnover; they should be considered by any college or university concerned about the effects of faculty working past age 70, including reduced faculty turnover and increased costs.**

Retirement incentive programs are specifically designed to encourage faculty turnover. They have been widely used in higher education and can significantly affect faculty retirement behavior. Colleges and universities can target such programs to fields or disciplines in which turnover is most needed, and they can limit participation to control both turnover and costs.

Accepting a retirement incentive must be voluntary, so such incentive programs and individual buyouts create additional retirement options for faculty, not forced retirements. They can offer faculty additional financial benefits and the opportunity to make a gradual transition to retirement. Whether these plans are money savers for the institution or are a way of exchanging a retirement problem for a financial one will depend on the institution's circumstances and actions. (In Chapter 5 we describe ways in which some institutions have taken costs into account when offering these programs.)

The committee emphasizes that retirement incentive programs and individual retirement incentive contracts must be entered into freely and without coercion, when seen by both the institution and the individual as beneficial. Although it is unlikely that a college or university would tie a retirement agreement to the granting of tenure, in order to avoid the possibility of coercion, colleges and universities should limit offers of retirement incentive programs or individualized retirement incentives to tenured faculty.

It is also inappropriate to ask a faculty member to decide whether a retirement incentive offer would be beneficial when retirement is only a remote prospect. Therefore, colleges and universities should offer retirement incentive programs and individual buyouts only to faculty ready to consider seriously when to retire. We believe 50 is an appropriate minimum age. Moreover, since these programs and buyouts are commonly designed for faculty in their 60s, by extending the opportunity to participate in retirement incentive programs to tenured faculty aged 50 and over, colleges and universities could benefit by increasing turnover and in planning for faculty retirements.

**The committee recommends that colleges and universities offer retirement incentive programs and individual retirement incentive contracts only to tenured faculty aged 50 and over.**

Congress has clearly authorized retirement incentive programs that include a minimum age for participation, that are offered for a window of time, and that provide bridge payments until retirees are eligible for Social Security. However, the legal status of some features of retirement incentive programs may still need clarification; Congress and the responsible federal agencies could assist colleges and universities by clearly preserving several options.

**The committee recommends that Congress, the Internal Revenue Service, and the Equal Employment Opportunity Commission permit colleges and universities to offer faculty voluntary retirement incentive programs that: are not classified as an employee benefit, include an upper age limit for participants, and limit participation on the basis of institutional needs.**

## Pensions

We believe that financial concerns should not be pivotal in faculty retirement decisions. Faculty pension, health insurance, and other retirement policies should create neither disincentives to retirement nor inadvertent incentives to postpone retirement.

**We recommend that colleges and universities offer pension plans designed to provide retired faculty with a continuing retirement income from all sources equal to between 67 and 100 percent of their preretirement income.**

Actual pension incomes vary depending on institutional policies and market performance. Furthermore, individual pensions may be based on service at more than one institution or outside academia. In some cases faculty can choose how to invest their retirement contributions, so an individual faculty member's pension will depend on the rates of return of his or her investment choices. Thus, our recommendation is for upper and lower bounds to guide pension contribution policies, rather than a single target percentage of preretirement income.

**The committee recommends that TIAA-CREF, other private pension plan providers, and state retirement systems work with institutions of higher education to develop pension plans that provide continuing retirement incomes within the committee's suggested range.**

We suggest a maximum as well as a minimum goal for inflation-protected pension income in the interest of best allocating scarce resources and limiting inadvertent incentives to postpone retirement. We found that faculty at some universities with generous pension plans, usually of the defined contribution type, could increase their pension income by 10-14 percent, or several thousand dollars, by postponing retirement for 1 year. If colleges and universities save any funds by limiting institutional pension contributions, they can redirect them to other benefits for retired faculty, such as health benefits and programs for retirees.

Colleges and universities could limit their contributions to a pension plan in several ways not requiring congressional or regulatory action. Colleges and universities with defined contribution plans are less able to limit the cost of their pension programs. Institutions that offer defined benefit plans can limit their contributions on the basis of years of service or a maximum percentage of preretirement salary. Institutions that offer hybrid plans—that is, plans with both defined contribution and defined benefit components—can limit their contributions to the defined benefit component. Colleges and universities with defined contributions plans are less able to limit the cost of their pension programs. Institutions that offer defined contribution plans can convert their plans to defined benefit plans or hybrid plans, although the administrative difficulties of conversion and the disadvantages of defined benefit plans may outweigh the benefits (see Chapter 4). Although legal violations are, of course, determined by the courts, Congress and the agencies responsible for interpreting pension regulations could assist colleges and universities by clarifying the laws and regulations governing limits to contributions in defined contribution plans.

**The committee recommends that Congress, the Internal Revenue Service, and the Equal Employment Opportunity Commission adopt poli-**

cies allowing employers to limit contributions to defined contribution plans on the basis of estimated level of pension income.

Our recommendation is for a *continuing* level of income. A pension income will continue to be adequate over the course of a retirement only when protected against inflation. The committee believes that further study of indexed investments is needed, and it urges the IRS to examine the costs and benefits of regulations that would make indexed investments available. We also encourage pension plan providers to consider them as a means of protecting pension incomes from inflation.

Because this option is not now available, we urge states and colleges and universities to offer defined benefit plans that provide retirees with cost-of-living adjustments that reflect the inflation rate. We encourage faculty covered by defined contribution plans to take advantage of annuity payment options designed to adjust for inflation. Lastly, we encourage the organizations that administer defined contribution plans to seek better ways to protect pension incomes from inflation.

### Health Benefits

Inadequate or expensive retirement health coverage creates a disincentive to retirement. Institutions can give retirees additional financial security by providing retirement health care coverage. Institutions can share the cost of retirement health care with retirees by allowing them to remain in college or university group insurance plans at their own expense.

The committee recommends that administrators and faculty seek affordable ways to improve retirees' medical coverage, such as redirecting funds from other retirement benefit programs or establishing tax-sheltered health savings plans for faculty to save for their own retirement health costs.

We note, however, that the national health care cost crisis cannot be resolved entirely within the framework of higher education. The rising cost of medical care creates financial concerns not only for faculty, retired faculty, and institutions of higher education but for people and institutions in all sectors of the economy.

### Faculty Perquisites for Retirees and Retirement Planning Assistance

Faculty members who are considering retirement may be reluctant to give up regular contact with students and colleagues or such faculty privileges as access to a laboratory or library. Colleges and universities can offer some continued faculty perquisites as a way to make retirement more attractive. At the same time, retired faculty can continue to contribute to the life of their college or university. Many perquisites, such as office space, entail significant costs to colleges and universities, but others, such as invitations to events, involve little or no marginal cost.

**The committee recommends that colleges and universities seek opportunities for retired faculty to maintain their contacts with colleagues, students, the institution, and their field of scholarship.**

Retirement planning assistance can ease the transition to retirement and make retirement a more attractive option. Ideally, faculty members should know about retirement options throughout their careers, consider retirement options in the context of their individual needs, and be able to learn from others' experiences with retirement. In addition to the services offered by pension plan providers, ways to do this include assigning an individual or office to coordinate retirement planning and reimbursing faculty for the services of outside retirement planners.

**The committee recommends that all colleges and universities assist their faculty in planning for retirement.**

## THE ADEA EXEMPTION

In creating a series of exemptions for higher education in age discrimination legislation, Congress recognized the special nature of higher education. Congress responded to concerns that, without mandatory retirement, tenure and low turnover could make it difficult for colleges and universities to hire new faculty as a source of new ideas and new research fields. The committee believes that if colleges and universities—with assistance from Congress and regulatory agencies, states, and pension plan providers—vigorously pursue the recommendations in this report, all but a few institutions of higher education will adjust to the elimination of mandatory retirement without significant effects. For those few universities at which a high proportion of faculty members are most likely to work past age 70, the greatest adverse effects will occur during an initial adjustment period when turnover will be most reduced. These universities in particular will need the congressional and regulatory actions we recommend: clarifying retirement incentive options and revising pension policies.

The committee also believes that some aspects of eliminating mandatory retirement are clearly beneficial. Most obviously, faculty gain freedom in deciding when to retire. Eliminating mandatory retirement would also be in keeping with the general intent of the Age Discrimination in Employment Act to extend protection against age discrimination.

In this report the committee has examined a number of practical steps that are available or could be made available to address the problems raised by the elimination of mandatory retirement.

**The committee recommends that Congress and regulatory agencies, states and pension plan providers, and colleges and universities take these practical steps.**

**Given that these steps can be taken, there is no strong basis for continuing the exemption for tenured faculty.**

**The committee recommends that the ADEA exemption permitting the mandatory retirement of tenured faculty be allowed to expire at the end of 1993.**

# Appendix A

# Description of Study Methods

In evaluating the potential effects of eliminating mandatory retirement for tenured faculty, the committee reviewed available evidence in three broad areas of concern: (1) faculty demographics and retirement behavior, (2) the effects of aging on faculty performance, and (3) financial and legal issues. The committee undertook a range of research activities relevant to all three areas as well as activities specific to each area. Table A-1 shows the committee's activities and their relationship to the issues covered in the report. This appendix briefly describes each of the activities.

In planning, conducting, and assessing the results of the activities described in this appendix, committee members drew on their own years of experience as faculty, administrators, and trustees at a wide range of colleges and universities (see Appendix D). This experience was an essential element in the committee's deliberations and in the formulation of this report.

## ACTIVITIES RELEVANT TO ALL AREAS OF THE STUDY

Several of the committee's activities were designed to address faculty retirement issues relevant to all areas of substantive interest. The most important of these was the seven 2-day meetings over a 15-month period at which the committee planned its study, oversaw its execution, and reached consensus on the results. The other activities relevant to all areas of the study served two general purposes: (1) to identify the full range of mandatory retirement issues in higher education and (2) to understand how faculty and higher education institutions make retirement policies and personal retirement decisions. They included preliminary site visits, presentations from interested organizations, letters from administrators and faculty, case studies, and a review of faculty retirement laws.

TABLE A-1   Committee Activities

| Activity | Faculty Demographics and Behavior | Aging, Tenure, and Evaluation | Financial and Legal Issues |
|---|:---:|:---:|:---:|
| Committee meetings (seven 2-day meetings) | • | • | • |
| Presentations to committee: AARP, AAU, AAUP, ACE, AFT, NASULGC, NEA, AACJC, AAMC, EEOC[a] | • | | |
| Letters of inquiry | | | |
| Campus presidents | • | • | • |
| Heads of faculty | • | • | • |
| State faculty retirement laws | | | • |
| Faculty retirement laws of other countries | | | • |
| Case studies | • | • | • |
| Workshops | | | |
| Faculty demographics and modeling | • | | |
| Aging and performance | | • | |
| Financial and legal issues | | | • |
| Commissioned papers | | | |
| Employee pension and benefit law | | | • |
| Retirement incentives and antidiscrimination law | | | • |
| Law pertaining to tenure, dismissal, and evaluation | | • | • |
| Costs of retirement incentive programs | | | • |
| Programs for retirees | | | • |
| Analyses of data and literature | | | |
| Faculty data bases and faculty retirement research | • | | |
| Aging and faculty performance evaluation | | • | |
| Benefit plans and retirement incentive programs | | | • |

[a]See text for full names.

We began with a series of preliminary site visits. In the summer of 1989, prior to the committee's first meeting, the chair and staff visited six campuses and three multicampus system headquarters to talk with a few faculty and administrators about what issues, if any, they believed were raised by the possibility of eliminating mandatory retirement. During these visits we obtained the views of more than 30 administrators and faculty members, which were summarized for committee members at the first meeting.

The 1986 amendments to the Age Discrimination in Employment Act called on the U.S. Equal Employment Opportunity Commission (EEOC) to sponsor the committee's study. The amendments also named seven independent organizations especially interested in the committee's study:

American Association of Retired Persons
American Association of University Professors
American Council on Education
American Federation of Teachers
Association of American Universities
National Association of State Universities and Land Grant Colleges
National Education Association

The committee invited the EEOC and these groups to send a representative to attend a committee meeting to present the agency's and the organizations' perspectives on mandatory retirement issues in higher education. In addition, the committee requested presentations from two other groups with special perspectives on faculty retirement policies and access to faculty retirement data: the American Association of Community and Junior Colleges and the Association of American Medical Schools. The committee found these presentations informative and helpful in identifying issues and as sources of information.

The committee sent a letter of inquiry to a sample of college and university presidents and faculty, soliciting their views on key issues related to mandatory retirement. The committee developed a list of issues on the basis of presentations of preliminary site visits and members' own experience as faculty members, administrators, and trustees:

- impact on hiring young faculty members;
- impact on hiring women and minority faculty members;
- reduction of faculty supply because of perceptions of a tight market;
- effect on faculty quality and individual performance;
- impact on ability to upgrade departments;
- impact on ability to keep good people;
- disciplines that would be seriously affected;
- cost to the institution for early retirement incentives;
- cost to the institution for large contributions to the retirement program;

• limited flexibility to meet emerging opportunities;
• limited ability to reward personal growth, to cushion any decline in enrollment, and to plan transitions;
  • impact on availability of faculty housing;
  • ability to continue work and contributions;
  • deterioration in department's environment, (i.e., less stimulating);
  • effects on tenure rules;
  • preservation of financial options for individual faculty members; and
  • implications for performance evaluation.

Committee staff drew a sample of 358 colleges and universities stratified by the six broad institutional classifications developed by the Carnegie Foundation for the Advancement of Teaching (see Appendix C for a more detailed discussion of the classifications). In order to ensure an adequate response from research universities, the sample included the 50 universities with the largest research and development spending and 12 other universities among the 50 institutions that grant the most doctorates annually but are not among the top 50 in research and development expenditures. The committee invited the presidents of each of the colleges and universities in the sample to comment on the list of issues included with the letter, to identify other important mandatory retirement issues, and to give their views on any other related topics.

The committee also wanted to obtain the views of faculty members. Staff contacted each of the colleges and universities sampled to obtain the name and address of the head of the faculty senate or equivalent organization. The committee then sent a letter of inquiry and list of issues to faculty representatives at the 216 institutions at which such a person could be identified (142 of the 358 colleges and universities sampled reported they did not have a faculty senate or its equivalent).

The committee sent follow-up letters and made phone calls to presidents and faculty representatives who did not respond to the initial letter. By the time the committee received its last letter in July 1990, more than 70 percent of the presidents and 40 percent of the faculty representatives had responded. We believe the difference in response rates between the two groups reflects the relatively greater administrative resources associated with the office of president and other logistical challenges in formulating a faculty response.

The committee learned a great deal from the letters and by reviewing simple tabulations of issues mentioned in the responses. Among both presidents and faculty representatives, those from research universities were most likely to predict problems associated with the elimination of mandatory retirement; those from comprehensive and liberal arts colleges were least likely to predict difficulties. Many faculty senate heads believed that, on the whole, faculty would benefit from the elimination of mandatory retirement. Some tempered their remarks by predicting that uncapping could lead to greater use of performance evaluation and could lead some institutions to question the continuing value of the tenure system.

Many of the letters reflected thoughtful consideration of the issues. The committee found the letters useful in understanding the range of opinions in academia on issues related to mandatory retirement, and it drew on letter responses in developing its other activities. Comments from the letters are used to illustrate the committee's findings in the body of the report.

As a way to supplement available information on how colleges and universities set retirement policies and how faculty make retirement decisions, the committee conducted case studies of 17 colleges and universities selected to represent a range of institutional types. (We refer to these institutions by their Carnegie category since we agreed not to report their names.) Although we could not hope to represent fully the more than 3,200 colleges and universities in the United States with a small number of case studies, the committee balanced its choice of case study institutions by type (i.e., different Carnegie categories), enrollment, geographic region, and control (public or private). The committee also selected some case study institutions on the basis of more specialized factors it wished to explore, such as historically black institutions, women's colleges, and private colleges affiliated with a church. Selections were based partly on exploratory site visits and letter survey responses, although not all case study institutions were part of the letter survey sample.

Prior to each visit the committee asked the case study institution to provide the age distribution of its faculty, recent faculty retirement ages, data on faculty salaries by age, information on university or college retirement benefit policies, and, if relevant, retirement incentive programs and faculty evaluation policies. Staff, usually accompanied by committee members, visited each case study institution for 1 to 3 days, conducting a series of intensive, open-ended interviews with faculty and administrators. Following each campus visit, the site team confirmed its findings with the case study institution.

The committee collected information on state laws governing faculty retirement ages and on laws governing faculty retirement in other industrial nations. The committee sent letters to the attorneys general in all 50 states, the District of Columbia, and Puerto Rico, asking whether state law prohibited mandatory retirement of faculty at public or private colleges and universities in the state. Letters were followed where necessary with telephone calls to the attorney general's office or other state authorities to which the attorney general referred the inquiry—in most cases the state board of higher education or state university system office. If state offices could only verify that the state had or had not eliminated mandatory retirement for public institutions, we also contacted a sample of private colleges and universities in the state to confirm the presence or absence of a state law eliminating mandatory retirement for faculty at private institutions. The committee was also able to draw on the results of an independent survey of mandatory retirement policies at public 4-year colleges and universities (Wilner, 1990). Figure 2 contains the results of this inquiry.

The committee also reviewed the published literature on faculty retirement in other industrialized nations and sent a letter to faculty organizations in other countries requesting information on laws and rules governing faculty retirement (the American Association of University Professors provided a mailing list for this purpose). Of the five faculty organizations responding, four reported mandatory retirement ages below age 70 and the fifth, Canada, reported that some provinces had no mandatory retirement age, but the courts were reviewing the issue. The committee also learned that as part of the perestroika reforms, the Soviet Union had instituted a mandatory retirement age of 65 for senior scientists.

## FACULTY DEMOGRAPHICS AND RETIREMENT BEHAVIOR

In order to understand current faculty retirement behavior and to assess the impact of possible changes in faculty retirement ages when mandatory retirement is eliminated, the committee held a workshop and carried out several special analyses.

The workshop on faculty demographics and modeling brought members of the committee together with experts on higher education labor markets, faculty supply and demand modeling, and faculty data bases. Participants at the workshop discussed how faculty data bases might be used to gain an understanding of tenured faculty retirement patterns. The attendees were

Jay Chronister, Center for the Study of Higher Education, University of Virginia

Robert Dauffenbach, Office of Business and Economic Research, Oklahoma State University

Alan Fechter, Office of Scientific and Engineering Personnel, National Research Council

Michael Finn, Office of Scientific and Engineering Personnel, National Research Council

Robert Jones, Institutional Planning Office, American Association of Medical Colleges

Charlotte Kuh, Graduate Record Examination Board

Robert McGinnis, Cornell Institute for Social and Economic Research

On the basis of the workshop results, the committee undertook an analysis of available data bases on faculty age distributions and retirement ages. The committee also reviewed the research literature focusing on faculty retirement behavior, including recently completed and ongoing studies (e.g., Lozier and Dooris, 1988, 1989, and 1990; Rees and Smith, 1991).

The committee also requested faculty retirement data from colleges and universities in states that have eliminated mandatory retirement for tenured faculty and from other institutions selected because the committee's research suggested their retirement patterns would be of interest. This latter group included a number of research universities.

In order to estimate the effects of eliminating mandatory retirement on costs and faculty turnover, the committee made use of faculty flow models and data from three research universities. In two cases the university used its own model and data on its faculty age distribution, hiring patterns, and retirement behavior to project the effects of different assumptions about the proportion of faculty likely to work past age 70 if permitted to do so. In the third case the university provided faculty data and assumptions about the number of faculty likely to work past age 70, and staff analyzed the data using a model based on Biedenweg and Keenan (1989).

## FACULTY AGING, PERFORMANCE EVALUATION, AND TENURE

The committee examined research on the effects of aging on faculty teaching and scholarship, the use of various types of performance evaluations in assessing teaching and scholarship, and the effects on tenure of eliminating mandatory retirement.

The committee held a workshop for experts on aging and its effects. Discussion topics included research on the relationship between age and physiological and cognitive changes, aging and employment, and faculty aging. The committee drew on the results of this workshop as it conducted subsequent activities in this area. The attendees were

Jeanne Bader, University of Minnesota
James Birren, University of California, Los Angeles
Howard Freeman, University of California, Los Angeles
Steve Scallen, University of Minnesota
K. Warner Schaie, Pennsylvania State University
Sharon Smith, Project on Faculty Retirement, Princeton University
Harvey Sterns, University of Akron
Ellen Switkes, University of California
Steven Weiland, University of Minnesota

The committee analyzed the research literature on aging and performance in general and, when information was available, on aging and faculty teaching and research performance. Drawing in part on a parallel effort by the Committee on Performance Appraisal (National Research Council, 1991), the committee also assessed research on performance evaluation. As part of a set of commissioned legal papers, the committee asked Arval Morris of the University of Washington School of Law to prepare a monograph on legal issues pertaining to tenure and faculty dismissal for unsatisfactory performance. Morris surveyed and analyzed laws and cases on tenure and faculty dismissal.

## FINANCIAL AND LEGAL ISSUES

The committee recognized that college and university policies affect faculty retirement behavior, and the rules and regulations governing those policies partly determine how colleges and universities can respond to the elimination of mandatory retirement. Therefore, the committee conducted a number of activities focused on financial and legal aspects of college and university governance.

The workshop on financial and legal issues gave committee members the opportunity to discuss legal and financial issues with experts in university finance, management, and governance. Workshop participants discussed pension plans, health benefits, retirement incentive programs, continued perquisites for retirees, and the effects of these programs on institutional budgets and faculty retirement decisions. The attendees were

Albert Bowker, President Emeritus, City University of New York

Paul Boymel, Equal Employment Opportunity Commission

Deborah Chollet, Employee Benefit Research Institute

Jay Chronister, Center for the Study of Higher Education, University of Virginia

Craig Daniels, School of Arts and Sciences, Eastern Connecticut State University

Joyce Fescke, Vice President for Human Resources, DePaul University

Frederick Ford, Executive Vice President and Treasurer, Purdue University

Katherine Hanson, Consortium on Financing Higher Education

Francis King, Teachers Insurance and Annuity Association-College Retirement Equities Fund

David Lewin, Director of Personnel Services, University of Kansas

James Mauch, Professor of Administrative and Policy Studies, University of Pittsburgh

Judith McMorrow, School of Law, Washington and Lee University

Diane Oakley, Teachers Insurance and Annuity Association-College Retirement Equities Fund

Thomas O'Brien, School of Management, University of Massachusetts, Amherst

Joseph Pettit, Vice President for Planning and Institutional Research, Georgetown University

Robert Scott, Vice President for Finance, Harvard University

Neil Smelser, University Professor, University of California

Sharon Smith, Project on Faculty Retirement, Princeton University

Harvey Sterns, Institute for Life Span Development and Gerontology, University of Akron

Charles Stewart, Jones, Day, Reavis and Pogue, Washington, D.C.

Robert Wilson, Vice President for Personnel Programs, Johns Hopkins University

Robert Zemsky, Institute for Research on Higher Education, University of Pennsylvania

Working with the American Association of University Professors and the American Association of Universities, the committee commissioned three papers on legal issues relevant to mandatory retirement. One was the paper by Arval Morris noted above. The second, by Lee Irish and Charles Stewart of Jones, Day, Reavis and Pogue, covered institutional responses to the elimination of mandatory retirement. This paper examined employee pension and benefit laws and regulations as they affect faculty pension plans and retirement incentive programs. The third paper, by Judith McMorrow of Washington and Lee University, covered federal age discrimination laws and regulations and their effects on retirement incentive plans.

As part of its workshop on financial and legal issues, the committee commissioned two background papers: "Characteristics and Costs Related to the Provision of Incentive Early Retirement Plans for Faculty," by Jay Chronister of the University of Virginia, and "Looking Forward to Uncapping: A Pilot Inquiry into Costs of Faculty Retirement Benefits and Inducements," by James Mauch of the University of Pittsburgh.

The committee marshalled and assessed information about the characteristics of higher education benefit plans, including pension programs, retirement health benefits, retirement incentive programs, and other retirement benefits, such as retirement planning assistance and perquisites for retirees. The committee supplemented its review of the literature on higher education benefit programs with information from pension plan providers, including TIAA-CREF and several state retirement systems, and from individual colleges and universities.

# Appendix B

# Discussion of National Faculty Data Bases

The figures in Chapter 2 showing the age distribution of faculty members are based on data from three surveys: the National Survey of Postsecondary Faculty (NSOPF), conducted by the National Center for Education Statistics of the U.S. Department of Education; the Survey of Doctorate Recipients (SDR), conducted by the National Research Council for the National Science Foundation and other federal sponsors; and the faculty survey conducted by the Higher Education Research Institute (HERI) of the University of California at Los Angeles. The NSOPF and the SDR also provide data on the age distribution of faculty members by type of institution and by academic field. The HERI data provide information from a larger number of faculty members, although faculty were included in that survey using nonscientific sampling techniques. The HERI faculty age distribution, which looks similar to the NSOPF and SDR age profiles, was included because so few large faculty data bases are available. In this appendix we describe the three data bases used; Table A-2 shows the basic characteristics of each.

## THE SURVEY OF DOCTORATE RECIPIENTS

The SDR is a longitudinal survey of doctorate holders in the sciences, social sciences, engineering, and humanities. It is designed to collect information on the demographics, employment, and supply of those doctorate holders in the United States. As the most recent SDR methodological report (National Research Council, 1989a:1) describes the survey:

> The SDR project has surveyed doctoral scientists and engineers on a biennial basis since 1973 and humanities doctorate recipients since 1977; it includes in its data files historical information on employment status, employment sector, primary work activity, academic rank and tenure status,

TABLE A-2   Characteristics of National Faculty Data Bases

| Survey | Year Data Collected | Sample Composition | Response (percent) | Number[a] |
|---|---|---|---|---|
| Survey of Doctorate Recipients (SDR) | 1973-1989 | Doctorate holders[b] | 54.9 | 19,117[c] |
| National Survey of Postsecondary Faculty (NSOPF) | 1988 | All faculty | 76 | 8,383 |
| Higher Education Research Institute (HERI) | 1989 | All faculty | 55[d] | 51,574 |

[a]Number of faculty providing usable response.
[b]Excluding doctorate recipients in education and professional fields.
[c]Number of respondents who reported they were faculty.
[d]Responses not from a random sample of faculty.

and salary. The longitudinal nature of the survey—that is, individual members of the survey panel are resurveyed every two years—makes it possible to track the career patterns of survey participants and estimate field, work activity, and sectoral mobility among highly specialized personnel.

The SDR sample population is selected from all research doctorates granted in the United States. The total sample size for the 1989 survey was 91,327; 48,408 usable responses were received. Our age distribution tables and figures are based on the replies of 19,117 doctorate holders reporting employment as faculty members.

Since the SDR is a survey of doctorate recipients, it is not representative of all faculty. In particular, we did not use the SDR to estimate the age distribution of faculty at 2-year colleges because approximately 75 percent of 2-year college faculty do not have doctorates. The SDR is more representative of the faculty at 4-year colleges and universities, about 70 percent of whom have doctorates.

Prior to 1987 individuals were selected for the sample who had earned their doctorates within the past 42 years. For each new survey the oldest two groups were dropped and replaced by a sample of people who had received doctorates in the previous 2 years, thus maintaining the 42-year coverage span. In 1987 and 1989, in response to concern about the retirement rates of doctorate holders, the oldest groups were retained in the sample when new doctorate recipients were added. Thus, the 1989 sample contained individuals who received a doctorate between January 1, 1942, and June 30, 1988 (National Research Council, 1989a; 1990b).

The exclusion from the sample of individuals earning doctorates prior to 1942, reflecting the survey's original intent "to represent all working-age doctorates living in the United States" (National Research Council, 1990b:2), creates a possible source of bias in measuring the number of doctorate holders or faculty over age 70. According to SDR statistics, the median age at which doctorate holders earned their degrees in 1942 was 28, so the majority of faculty earning doctorates in 1942 would have been in their 70s at the time of the 1989 survey. Therefore, we believe any error in the age distribution of employed faculty resulting from the absence of individuals earning doctorates prior to 1942 is likely to be small.

The SDR has been conducted as a mail survey since it began. Response rates have declined from 75 percent for the first survey in 1973 to 55 percent in 1989. As the response rate decreases, the probability increases that the data received do not accurately represent the population. (For a detailed discussion of the need to improve the SDR response rate, see National Research Council, 1989b.) The low response rate for recent surveys gave the committee additional reason for caution in using SDR results. We note that a 1989 pilot study of the effectiveness of computer-assisted telephone interviewing as a way to obtain interviews from nonrespondents to the mail survey suggests that improvement in the overall response rate is possible (National Research Council, 1990b), and we commend efforts to increase the response rate in order to make the SDR more useful for future researchers.

When faculty respondents to the SDR are divided into subcategories by age and institution type or field, the unweighted numbers of faculty over age 60 in some categories drop below 50. The unweighted numbers of faculty aged 65-69 and 70 or older in some fields are single digits or zero. The committee therefore limited its analysis of faculty age distributions to broad fields of study and broad categories of institutional types. We view the data on the proportion of older faculty by field with some caution. The committee also checked the data on faculty age distribution by institution type and field against results from the NSOPF. In Chapter 2 we present results only from the SDR, since the NSOPF has a smaller sample size and therefore requires similar caution.

The SDR is not very useful for looking at retirement issues. The number of faculty responding that they were employed in 1987 and retired in 1989 was too low for us to calculate retirement rates. The survey asks only for current employment status, not for when that status changed. Therefore, the data show only that a respondent's retirement occurred sometime between the last survey on which he or she reported employment and the first on which he or she reported retirement. For individuals responding to consecutive surveys, this would give a 2-year range of possible retirement ages. However, respondents checking "retired" who did not respond to the previous survey may have retired during the previous 4 or more years.

Although the SDR is a longitudinal survey, many respondents do not respond in successive survey years: For example, only about 65 percent of the 1989 survey respondents also responded in 1987.

Furthermore, the SDR survey form is not designed to collect information on retirement from a specific job, such as a tenured faculty position. It asks respondents to indicate whether they are employed full time, employed part time, on a postdoctoral appointment, unemployed and seeking full-time or part-time employment, not employed and not seeking employment, or retired and not employed. Faculty who officially retire and continue to work part time as part of a partial retirement program or faculty who engage in research or consulting work after retiring from a tenured position might therefore not indicate their retirement on the survey form.

## NATIONAL SURVEY OF POSTSECONDARY FACULTY

The NSOPF is a survey of instructional faculty in higher education; the National Center for Education Statistics (NCES) conducted this study for the first time during the 1987-1988 academic year. The NSOPF had three components: a survey of institutional policies and practices, which was sent to institutions; a survey of faculty at those institutions; and a survey of department chairs at those institutions. Faculty provided information on their backgrounds, responsibilities, compensation, and attitudes. Institutional and department-level respondents provided information on faculty composition, turnover, recruitment, retention, and tenure policies (National Center for Education Statistics, 1990b).

The stratified random sample of 480 institutions used in the survey was selected (National Center for Education Statistics, 1990b:94): " . . . [from all] accredited nonproprietary U.S. postsecondary institutions that grant a two-year (A.A.) or higher degree and whose accreditation at the higher education level is recognized by the U.S. Department of Education. " The sample included religious colleges, medical schools that are independent of a 4-year college or university, other specialized postsecondary institutions, and 2- and 4-year colleges and universities. The sample was drawn from the 1987 Integrated Postsecondary Education Data System (IPEDS), which contained 3,159 institutions meeting the sample criteria (National Center for Education Statistics, 1990b).

Of the 480 institutions in the sample, 449 (94 percent) provided lists of their part-time and full-time instructional faculty members. A stratified random sample of 12,569 faculty was selected from these lists. On the basis of the responses received, NCES estimated that 11,071 of the respondents met eligibility criteria as regular instructional faculty; 8,382 eligible faculty responded, for a faculty response rate of 76 percent (National Center for Education Statistics, 1990b). This response rate does not take into account the 6 percent of sampled institutions that declined to participate and whose faculty were therefore not included.

## COMPARISON OF THE NSOPF AND SDR

The NSOPF included questions asking faculty whether they anticipated retiring within the next 3 years, but because the survey population included current faculty only, the NSOPF produced no actual data on faculty retirements. Consequently, the committee chose to limit its use of NSOPF data, as it did the SDR data, to showing the age distribution of current faculty.

The NSOPF has two advantages over the SDR as a source of data on faculty members. First, it is a survey of faculty, rather than of doctorate holders, and it is therefore more representative of the population of faculty members. Second, its sample design did not contain any selection criteria likely to exclude the oldest faculty, such as the exclusion from the SDR of individuals who earned doctorates prior to 1942.

The NSOPF also has two disadvantages for the purposes of collecting information on faculty demographics. First, since the 1987-1988 survey was the first conducted, the NSOPF could not provide information on changes in faculty age distributions over time. The NCES has announced plans to repeat the survey in the 1991-1992 academic year, and the committee notes that in the future this survey may be a useful source of information on changes in faculty demographics, activities, and attitudes and in institutional policies.

Second, despite its higher response rate, the NSOPF provides data on fewer faculty than the SDR. As in the SDR, the number of faculty in the highest age categories is small, which limits analysis of the data by age and any other category such as type of institution or field of study. Further research on the demographics, responsibilities, and attitudes of older faculty would be possible if the 1991-1992 NSOPF oversampled faculty over age 60 in order to obtain a larger number of responses from older faculty members.

## HIGHER EDUCATION RESEARCH INSTITUTE
## FACULTY SURVEY

The HERI was conducted in 1989 with funding from the National Science Foundation, the Exxon foundation, and individual colleges and universities. It began as a survey of faculty at 150 colleges and universities, but the investigators then invited all the 2-year and 4-year colleges and universities in the country to participate in exchange for a fee to cover reporting data back to individual institutions. Thus, some institutions in the HERI survey were self-selected paying participants rather than part of a random sample chosen by standard statistical methods.

In all, 432 institutions participated. HERI asked institutions to provide a complete list of their faculty members; if the institution did not do so, HERI obtained lists of faculty from outside vendors. The lists obtained from both institutions and vendors reflect different institutional definitions of faculty status. Some included librarians, part-time faculty, and administrators in addition to regular full-time instructional faculty members. HERI distributed survey questionnaires to 93,479 faculty members listed and received 51,574 usable responses (55 percent).

The use of nonscientific sampling techniques limits the usefulness of HERI data, although HERI survey procedures contain no obvious sources of bias by age. The committee notes only that the age distribution of faculty responding to HERI is remarkably similar to the faculty age distributions calculated from SDR and NSOPF data. Since few large faculty data bases are available, we included the HERI age distribution in Chapter 2 as an additional check on the overall age distribution of U.S. faculty.

## RECOMMENDATIONS FOR FUTURE FACULTY SURVEYS

Modification of faculty surveys to provide additional data on faculty retirement behavior would assist policy makers at state and federal levels as well as those at colleges and universities not only in considering faculty retirement policy but also in predicting and preparing for possible changes in faculty supply and demand. The committee therefore recommends that the sponsors of faculty surveys oversample older faculty and, when relevant, retired faculty to ensure an adequate data base for estimating the number of faculty over age 70 and studying faculty retirement patterns. We also encourage survey sponsors to develop questions that measure when faculty retire and address such retirement issues as retirement benefits and factors affecting the decision to retire.

The committee notes that state retirement systems and private pension plan providers may also be in a position to collect data of use to government policy makers, colleges and universities, and researchers considering retirement issues. TIAA-CREF has already done a number of studies on retirement policy issues, including surveys of older and retired faculty members. However, the TIAA-CREF data base of participants and many state retirement system data bases do not contain any means of separating data on faculty from data on other participants in their pension plans. We recommend that pension plan providers seek ways to assist colleges and universities, policy makers, and researchers by coding data in a way that permits studies of faculty retirement behavior.

# Appendix C

# Characteristics of Institutions and Faculty

Many of the factors we consider in this report on faculty retirement—including faculty roles and performance, pension plans and other retirement benefits, institutional costs, and faculty needs—are not the same for the almost 300,000 tenured faculty members at more than 3,200 different colleges and universities. Faculty life differs not only among disciplines within an institution (e.g., whether work requires a laboratory) but also as a result of such characteristics as the proportion of full-time faculty, tenured faculty, and senior faculty; salary and fringe benefit levels; and whether the institution negotiates its faculty policies through collective bargaining. Consequently, the committee was aware that general trends in higher education will not have the same effect on all colleges and universities. Many factors affect this variation:

• *size of the institution*, with enrollments ranging from less than 200 to more than 50,000 students, and faculty sizes ranging from several dozen to several thousand;
• *origin*, from the oldest, Harvard, established in 1636 to train young men for the ministry, to more recent church-sponsored colleges, many also now secular; to the land grant colleges established under the 1861 Morrill Act; to the historically black colleges founded both before and after the Civil War; to former teacher-training colleges; to new institutions and branches of institutions serving newly developed or previously underserved areas;
• *control*, from colleges established and run by a church, to land grant institutions run by a state board of higher education, to private secular institutions whose trustees may be chosen from the local community or all over the world;
• *specialization*, from the International Bible College to the Colorado

School of Mines to Juillard and from the Massachusetts Institute of Technology to Oberlin College to the California State University system;

• *population served*, from community colleges serving students from the surrounding area, to private institutions and state colleges serving students from the state or from the region, to public and private universities attracting students from all over the country and all over the world;

• *location*, from Kodiak Community College (Alaska) to Hunter College (New York), from rural to urban areas, and from affluent to economically depressed areas; and

• *faculty characteristics, policies, and governance*, which include proportions of full-time and tenured faculty; salaries, which depend in part on control and location; and the way faculty are involved in institutional policy making, which can vary from informal contact with administrators, to formal presence on personnel and other committees, to collective bargaining processes.

For the purpose of understanding how trends and policies will affect faculty and institutions, we sought a way to classify the diverse range of college and universities into simple categories, such as public and private, highest degree offered, or range of subjects taught. We understand, however, that no such classification scheme will capture the diversity in higher education, and we agree with Clark (1987:21), who concludes:

> Even the most comprehensive classifications of institutions in American higher education must be seen as rough and ready. There is no one best way to define the boundaries of depicted types; in all schemes, odd bedfellows appear in most categories.

We decided to use the institutional classifications developed by the Carnegie Foundation for the Advancement of Teaching, which divide colleges and universities into categories by enrollment, subjects taught, number and types of degrees awarded, and the amount of outside research support received annually (*Chronicle of Higher Education*, July 8, 1987). There are 10 categories.

*Research Universities I* include 45 public and 25 private universities, among them Harvard, Massachusetts Institute of Technology, the University of California at Berkeley, Texas A&M, and the University of Florida. By Carnegie's definition:

> . . . [t]hese institutions offer a full range of baccalaureate programs, are committed to graduate education through the doctoral degree and give high priority to research. They receive annually at least $33.5 million in federal support for research and development and award at least 50 Ph.D. degrees each year.

*Research Universities II* include 26 public and 7 private universities, among them Georgetown University, the University of California at Santa Barbara, Florida State University, and Renssalaer Polytechnic Institute. Research Universities II, like Research Universities I, "offer a full range of baccalaureate programs, are committed to graduate education through the doctoral degree and give high priority to research." Also like Research Universities I, they award at least 50 Ph.D. degrees each year. Carnegie distinguishes Research Universities II from Research Universities I by level of research support: Research Universities II "receive annually between $12.5 million and $33.5 million in federal support for research and development."

The National Survey of Postsecondary Faculty (NSOPF) (see Appendix B) estimates that Research Universities I and II together employ 135,000 full-time instructional faculty members—28 percent of all full-time instructional faculty.

*Doctorate-Granting Universities I* include 29 public and 22 private universities, among them Tufts University, the University of California at Santa Cruz, and the University of Montana. According to Carnegie:

> In addition to offering a full range of baccalaureate programs, the mission of these institutions includes a commitment to graduate education through the doctoral degree. They award at least 40 Ph.D. degrees annually in five or more academic disciplines.

*Doctorate-Granting Universities II* include 34 public and 25 private universities, including Northern Arizona University, Pepperdine University, the Colorado School of Mines, and Drexel University. Like Doctorate I universities, they offer a full range of baccalaureate programs, and their mission includes a commitment to graduate education through the doctoral degree. Carnegie distinguishes them from Doctorate I universities by the number and variety of doctoral degrees granted: Doctorate-Granting Universities II "award annually 20 or more Ph.D. degrees in at least one discipline or 10 or more Ph.D. degrees in three or more disciplines." Doctorate-Granting Universities I and II together employ about 51,000 full-time instructional faculty—10 percent of all such faculty.

*Comprehensive Universities and Colleges I* include 285 public and 142 private institutions, among them the 19 universities in the California State University system, the University of Portland, Grambling State University, and Worcester Polytechnic Institute. By Carnegie's definition:

> . . . [t]hese institutions offer baccalaureate programs and, with few exceptions, graduate education through the master's degree. More than half of their baccalaureate degrees are awarded in two or more occupational or professional disciplines such as engineering or business administration. All of the institutions in this group enroll at least 2,500 full-time students.

*Comprehensive Universities and Colleges II* include 47 public and 127 private institutions, among them Jacksonville University, Illinois Wesleyan University, and the main campus of Southern Arkansas University. These institutions, like Comprehensive I institutions, award more than half their baccalaureate degrees in two or more occupational or professional disciplines, "and many also offer graduate education through the master's degree." In addition to this slight distinction in the number giving master's degrees, Carnegie distinguishes Comprehensive II institutions from Comprehensive I institutions by the number of students enrolled: Comprehensive II institutions all enroll between 1,500 and 2,500 full-time students. Approximately 128,000 full-time instructional faculty (26 percent) work at comprehensive institutions.

*Liberal Arts Colleges I* include 1 public and 124 private institutions, among them St. John's Colleges of Annapolis and Santa Fe, Amherst College, Oberlin College, and the State University of New York at Purchase. According to Carnegie, "[t]hese highly selective institutions are primarily undergraduate colleges that award more than half of their baccalaureate degrees in arts and science fields." Carnegie also includes in this category three institutions with a "liberal arts tradition" that meet the criteria for Doctorate-Granting University II: Bryn Mawr College, Wesleyan University, and Drew University.

*Liberal Arts Colleges II* include 30 public and 409 private institutions, among them Spelman College, Berry College, Oakland City College, and the University of Maine at Presque Isle. Carnegie defines Liberal Arts II institutions as

> primarily undergraduate colleges that are less selective and award more than half their degrees in liberal arts fields. This category also includes a group of colleges . . . that award *less* than half their degrees in liberal arts fields but, with fewer than 1,500 students, are too small to be considered comprehensive.

Liberal arts colleges tend to be small institutions. The NSOPF estimates that they employ 39,000 full-time instructional faculty—8 percent of all such faculty.

*Two-Year Colleges and Institutions* include 985 public and 383 private institutions, among them Santa Monica College, Sandhills Community College in North Carolina, Essex Community College in New Jersey, and the Katherine Gibbs School in Massachusetts. The Carnegie description of this category is brief: "These institutions offer certificate or degree programs through the Associate of Arts level and, with few exceptions, offer no baccalaureate degrees." About 95,000 full-time instructional faculty work at 2-year institutions—20 percent of all such faculty.

*Professional Schools and Other Specialized Institutions* include 66 public and 577 private institutions. Institutions in this category include separate medical schools and centers, such as the Uniformed Services University of the Health Sciences in Maryland; other schools for health professions, such as Mercer University Southern School of Pharmacy; independent law schools, such as the University of West Los Angeles; business schools, such as Fort Lauderdale College; engineering schools, such as the South Dakota School of Mines and Technology; schools of art, such as the School of the Art Institute of Chicago, and music, such as the New England Conservatory of Music; teachers colleges, such as Dr. Martin Luther King College in Minnesota; schools offering religious instruction, such as the American Indian Bible College in Arizona and Southwestern Baptist Theological Seminary; accredited corporate colleges and universities, such as the RAND Graduate School of Policy Studies; and other specialized institutions, such as the Massachusetts Maritime Academy. According to Carnegie, "[t]hese institutions offer degrees ranging from the bachelor's to the doctorate. At least 50 per cent of the degrees awarded by these institutions are in a single specialized field." More than 40,000 full-time instructional faculty work at specialized institutions—8 percent of all such faculty.

The Carnegie Foundation designed these categories as a typology of institutions, not a ranking. Even these broad categories are not based on obvious divisions: three institutions that meet the qualifications for both liberal arts colleges and doctoral universities are listed as liberal arts colleges in the most recent classification but were previously listed as doctoral universities. Classifications also change as institutions change; between 1972 and 1981, 592 institutions moved from one category to another (Clark, 1987:22). Clark (1987:20) observes:

> Liberal arts colleges become typed as comprehensive colleges when they take on more vocational programs. Institutions happily move out of [the comprehensive] category "up" into university status when they begin to give doctoral degrees and garner more research money.

Yet these movements do not imply any rank ordering of types. Clark (1987:20) goes on to observe that "[t]he top fifty liberal arts colleges are serious competitors for the best universities, public and private, in attracting talented students."

In considering not only the variation among categories of institutions but also the "odd bedfellows" within categories, the committee recognizes that the effects of eliminating mandatory retirement will vary from institution to institution within categories as well as between them. We therefore divide institutions by Carnegie categories only as a way of examining general trends linked to institutional type and of indicating basic characteristics of individual institutions. In most cases our discussion combines categories, referring to research universities, doctoral universities, comprehensive institutions, or liberal arts colleges, rather than distinguishing between Carnegie's two levels of each of these types.

We could not cover the entire range of institutions' faculty policies, but we can indicate some of the differences between institutions by showing the variation in selected factors by institutional type: Tables A-3 and A-4 show the distribution of institutions and faculty by such characteristics as academic degree, percent tenured, and salary. These characteristics are significant for retirement questions because they help determine an institution's faculty costs and its supply of new faculty members, including replacements for retirees. As the data on tenured faculty indicates, some institutions are outside the range of this study because they have no tenure system and no tenured faculty subject to mandatory retirement.

In discussing various institutional policies and possible changes in policies, the committee recognizes that colleges and universities have different policy-making procedures. They vary in level of faculty involvement in governance and in systems of faculty representation. Some of our policy recommendations apply to faculty representatives as well as to administrators, particularly at institutions with formal collective bargaining processes. Table A-5 shows the number of institutions with faculty unions by broad type of institution.

TABLE A-3 Faculty Characteristics by Type of Institution

| Type and Control of Institution | Number of Full-Time Faculty[a] | Full-Time Faculty with Ph.D. or First Professional Degree (percent) | Full-Time Faculty at Institutions Without a Tenure System (percent) | Full-Time Tenured Faculty at Institutions With a Tenure System | |
|---|---|---|---|---|---|
| | | | | Number | Percent |
| Public research | 96,228 | 90 | 1 | 66,000 | 68.9 |
| Private research | 39,136 | 93 | 2 | 21,000 | 54.3 |
| Public doctoral[b] | 53,871 | 82 | 0 | 23,000 | 64.6 |
| Private doctoral | 22,107 | 89 | 16 | 8,000 | 54.7 |
| Public comprehensive | 93,144 | 69 | 1 | 62,000 | 66.0 |
| Private comprehensive | 35,160 | 72 | 3 | 19,000 | 54.6 |
| Liberal arts | 39,086 | 62 | 13 | 19,000 | 50.6 |
| Public 2-year | 91,559 | 19 | 25 | 55,000 | 60.4 |
| Private 2-year[c] | | | | | |
| Medical[b] | | | | 11,000 | 44.7 |
| Other | 14,778 | 68 | 38 | 5,000 | 35.8 |
| Total | 489,164 | 67 | 9 | 292,000 | 59.7 |

[a]At all institutions with and without a tenure system.

[b]In the tabulations of the percent of faculty with Ph.D. or first professional degree, NCES combined doctoral institutions and institutions classified by the Carnegie Foundation as specialized medical schools.

[c]Too few cases for reliable estimates.

Sources: Data on faculty with Ph.D. or first professional degree and percent of faculty at institutions with a tenure system is from National Center for Education Statistics, (1990b:14). Data on faculty with tenure is from special National Survey of Postsecondary Faculty (NSOPF) tabulations prepared for this study by the National Center for Education Statistics.

TABLE A-4    Average Faculty Salaries, 1990-1991 (in dollars)

| Type of Institution and Faculty Rank | Type of Institutional Control | | | |
| --- | --- | --- | --- | --- |
| | Public | Private | Church | All |
| Research and doctoral institutions | | | | |
| Professor | 60,450 | 72,930 | 60,790 | 62,910 |
| Associate professor | 44,000 | 49,420 | 44,980 | 44,870 |
| Assistant professor | 36,980 | 41,640 | 38,030 | 37,820 |
| Instructor | 25,910 | 32,340 | 30,000 | 26,840 |
| Lecturer | 31,290 | 34,460 | 28,080 | 31,810 |
| All ranks | 47,650 | 57,320 | 47,520 | 49,320 |
| Comprehensive institutions | | | | |
| Professor | 52,190 | 52,820 | 51,180 | 52,180 |
| Associate professor | 41,570 | 41,050 | 40,700 | 41,390 |
| Assistant professor | 34,460 | 33,020 | 33,950 | 34,160 |
| Instructor | 26,170 | 24,250 | 27,310 | 25,980 |
| Lecturer | 26,500 | 28,380 | 33,560 | 26,920 |
| All ranks | 42,170 | 40,730 | 41,010 | 41,830 |
| Baccalaureate institutions | | | | |
| Professor | 44,900 | 49,610 | 40,040 | 44,570 |
| Associate professor | 37,550 | 38,200 | 33,080 | 35,980 |
| Assistant professor | 31,390 | 31,570 | 28,020 | 29,980 |
| Instructor | 26,510 | 25,470 | 23,600 | 24,760 |
| Lecturer | 27,110 | 32,840 | 22,470 | 28,030 |
| All ranks | 36,410 | 38,620 | 32,440 | 35,480 |
| 2-year institutions with academic ranks | | | | |
| Professor | 45,050 | 35,080 | 30,460 | 44,620 |
| Associate professor | 38,070 | 29,950 | 26,320 | 37,680 |
| Assistant professor | 31,870 | 27,150 | 23,300 | 31,470 |
| Instructor | 27,060 | 21,530 | 20,520 | 26,740 |
| Lecturer | 22,490 | [a] | [a] | 22,370 |
| All ranks | 36,420 | 28,280 | 25,320 | 35,960 |
| Total (institutions with academic ranks) | | | | |
| Professor | 55,830 | 61,620 | 47,240 | 56,210 |
| Associate professor | 42,210 | 43,280 | 37,540 | 41,780 |
| Assistant professor | 35,200 | 35,540 | 31,050 | 34,640 |
| Instructor | 26,330 | 26,240 | 24,800 | 26,090 |
| Lecturer | 29,310 | 33,190 | 27,690 | 29,930 |
| All Ranks | 44,020 | 47,010 | 37,270 | 43,720 |

*Note:* Salary figures are based on 2,127 institutions.

[a]Sample too small to be meaningful.

*Source:* Data from American Association of University Professors (1991:21).

TABLE A-5   Unionized Institutions by Type and Control

| Type of Institution | Number of Institutions (percent) | |
| --- | --- | --- |
| | Unionized | Not Unionized |
| 4-year public | 351 (62) | 215 (38) |
| 4-year private | 70 (5) | 1,389 (95) |
| 2-year public | 591 (63) | 344 (37) |
| 2-year private | 15 (4) | 356 (96) |

*Source:* Data from Douglas (1989:Table 10).

# Appendix D

# Biographical Sketches of Committee Members and Staff

**Ralph E. Gomory** (Chair) is president of the Alfred P. Sloan Foundation. He was Vice President for Science and Technology for the IBM Corporation and is a former IBM Fellow. He has served on departmental visiting committees and advisory councils at Harvard, Princeton, Stanford, and Yale Universities and the Massachusetts Institute of Technology and as a trustee of Hampshire College and Princeton University. He holds a B.A. degree from Williams College and a Ph.D. in mathematics from Princeton University. He is a member of the National Academy of Sciences, the National Academy of Engineering, and the President's Council of Advisors on Science and Technology. He was awarded the National Medal of Science in 1988.

**Norman M. Bradburn** is director of the National Opinion Research Center and Tiffany and Margaret Blake Distinguished Service Professor of behavioral science at the University of Chicago. Previously, he served as provost of the University of Chicago. He is a member of the Committee on National Statistics of the Commission on Behavioral and Social Sciences and Education at the National Research Council and serves as chair of its Board on International Comparative Studies in Higher Education. He holds B.A. degrees from the University of Chicago and Oxford University and M.A. and Ph.D. degrees in social psychology from Harvard University.

**David W. Breneman** is a visiting professor at the Graduate School of Education of Harvard University and former president of Kalamazoo College. He has recently completed a study of liberal arts colleges and is author and editor of several books, including *Academic Labor Markets and Careers* (with Ted I. K. Youn) and *Public Policy and Private Higher Edu-*

*cation* (with Chester E. Finn, Jr.). He previously served as a senior fellow of the Brookings Institution and as staff director of the National Board on Graduate Education at the National Research Council. He holds a B.A. from the University of Colorado and a Ph.D. in economics from the University of California at Berkeley.

**F. Albert Cotton** is Doherty-Welch Distinguished Professor of Chemistry at Texas A&M University and a member of the National Academy of Sciences. He has previously served on the faculty of the Massachusetts Institute of Technology. He has won several awards for his research, including a 1990 National Academy of Sciences award for outstanding contributions to science. He holds an A.B. from Temple University and a Ph.D. in chemistry from Harvard University.

**Pamela Ebert Flattau** is director of the Studies and Surveys Unit of Office of Scientific and Engineering Personnel at the National Research Council. She has worked as an NRC staff officer for a variety of studies within the Commission on Behavioral and Social Sciences and Education and the Commission on Human Resources and as a science policy analyst with the Science Indicators Unit of the National Science Foundation. She was an American Association for the Advancement of Science-American Psychological Association Congressional Science Fellow with the U.S. Senate Committee on Labor and Public Welfare, focusing on education policy issues. She holds a Ph.D. in experimental psychology from the University of Georgia.

**Dorothy M. Gilford** is director of the National Research Council's Board on International Comparative Studies in Education. Formerly, she served as director of the National Center for Education Statistics and as director of the mathematical sciences division of the Office of Naval Research. Her interests are in research program administration, organization of statistical systems, and education statistics. A fellow of the American Statistical Association, she has served as vice president of the association and chair of its committee on international relations in statistics. She received B.S. and M.S. degrees in mathematics from the University of Washington.

**Mary W. Gray** is a professor of mathematics, statistics, and computer science at the American University. She is also a member of the District of Columbia Bar and the American Bar Association. She served on the Commission on College Retirement, and she has served on many committees and boards of the American Association of University Professors, where she is currently chair of the Committee on the Status of Women in the Profession and a member of the Committees on Academic Freedom and Retirement. She received an A.B. degree in mathematics and physics from Hastings

College, M.A. and Ph.D. degrees in mathematics from the University of Kansas, and a J.D. from the American University.

**P. Brett Hammond** is director of Academy Studies at the National Academy of Public Administration. Previously, he served as Associate Executive Director of the Commission on Behavioral and Social Sciences and Education at the National Research Council. While at the NRC, he also served as a senior staff officer for studies on valuing health risks for regulatory decisions and evaluating sites for the superconducting supercollider. He holds B.A. degrees in economics and politics from the University of California at Santa Cruz and a Ph.D. in political science from the Massachusetts Institute of Technology.

**Donald C. Hood** is James F. Bender Professor of Psychology and a former Vice President for Arts and Sciences at Columbia University. He is a trustee of Smith College and is on the Faculty Planning Committee at Columbia. He is also a member of the National Research Council's Committee on Vision. He holds a B.A. in psychology and mathematics from Harpur College of the State University of New York at Binghamton and M.Sc. and Ph.D. degrees from Brown University.

**Harriet P. Morgan** served as research associate of the Committee on Mandatory Retirement in Higher Education. Her research interests include access to higher education and the structure of higher education systems. She holds a B.A. in public policy and economics from Duke University and an M.Sc. in social research and social policy from Oxford University.

**Robert M. O'Neil** is University Professor at the University of Virginia and director of the Thomas Jefferson Center for the Protection of Free Expression. He is former president of the University of Virginia and of the University of Wisconsin system. He serves on the boards of the Carnegie Foundation for the Advancement of Teaching, the Educational Testing Service, the Johnson Foundation, and the Commonwealth Fund. He holds A.B., A.M., and LL.B. degrees from Harvard University and LL.D. degrees from Indiana University and Beloit College.

**Robert E. Parilla** is president of Montgomery College, a three-campus community college system serving Montgomery County, Maryland. He has chaired the Statewide Committee on the Future of Maryland Community Colleges and the Maryland Council of Community College Presidents. He has also been a member of the American Council on Education's Commission on Leadership Development and Academic Administration and of the Committee to Study the Role of Allied Health Personnel of the Institute of Medicine. He holds a Ph.D. in higher education from Florida State University.

**Mitchell W. Spellman** is Dean Emeritus for International Projects and was formerly professor of surgery and Dean for Medical Services at Harvard Medical School. He has served on advisory committees and boards of visitors of medical schools at Duke University, the University of Michigan, Stanford University, and the University of California at Los Angeles; as a trustee of Occidental College; and as a member of the Georgetown University Board of Directors and the Massachusetts Institute of Technology Corporation. He also serves on the Board of Overseers of the Harvard Community Health Plan. He holds an A.B. from Dillard University, an M.D. from Howard University, and a Ph.D. in surgery from the University of Minnesota. He is a member of the Institute of Medicine.

# References

Albert, S.P.
1986 Retirement: From rite to rights. *Academe* (July-August):24-26.
American Association of University Professors
1983 Statement of the Wingspread conference on evaluation of tenured faculty. (AAUP Committee A on Academic Freedom and Tenure) *Academe* (November-December):14a.
1990 1940 Statement of Principles on Academic Freedom and Tenure with 1970 Interpretive Comments. *Policy Documents and Reports*. Washington, D.C.: American Association of University Professors.
1991 The Annual Report on the Economic Status of the Profession 1990-1991 *Academe* (March-April):Special Issue.
Astin, A.
1980 *When Does a College Deserve To Be Called "High Quality"*? Current Issues in Higher Education, No. 1. Washington, D.C.: American Association for Higher Education.
Astin, A., W. Korn, and E. Day
1991 *The American College Teacher: National Norms for the 1989-90 HERI Faculty Survey*. Los Angeles: Higher Education Research Institute, University of California at Los Angeles.
Atkinson, R.C.
1990 Supply and demand for scientists and engineers: A national crisis in the making. *Science* 248:425-432.
Baldwin, R.G., and R.T. Blackburn
1981 The academic career as a development process: Implications for higher education. *Journal of Higher Education* 52(6):598-614.
Bayer, A.E., and J.E. Dutton
1977 Career age and research professional activities of academic scientists: Tests of alternative nonlinear models and some implications for higher education faculty policies. *Journal of Higher Education* 48:259-82.

Biedenweg, R.
  1989  Faculty and facilities. In *The COHFE Faculty Planning Package*. Cambridge, Mass.: Consortium on Financing Higher Education.

Biedenweg, R., and T. Keenan
  1989  The faculty COHORT model. User manual. In *The COFHE Faculty Planning Package*. Cambridge, Mass.: Consortium on Financing Higher Education.

Blackburn, R.
  1972  Faculty Responsiveness and Faculty Productivity as Functions of Age, Rank, and Tenure: Some Inferences from the Empirical Literature. Educational Resources Information Center (ERIC) Report ED 059 703, Alexandria, Va.

Blackburn, R.T., and J. H. Lawrence
  1986  Aging and the quality of faculty job performance. *Review of Educational Research* 23(3):265-290.

Bowen, H.R., and J.H. Schuster
  1986  *American Professors: A National Resource Imperiled.* New York: Oxford University Press.

Bowen, W.G., G. Lord, and J.A. Sosa
  1991  Measuring time to the doctorate: Reinterpretation of the evidence. *Proceedings of the National Academy of Sciences* 88:713-717.

Bowen, W.G., and J.A. Sosa
  1989  *Prospects for Faculty in the Arts and Sciences: A Study of Factors Affecting Demand and Supply, 1987-2012.* Princeton, N.J.: Princeton University Press.

Burkhauser, R.V., and J.F. Quinn
  1989  An economywide view of changing mandatory retirement rules. Pp. 63-71 in K.C. Holden and W.L. Hansen, eds., *The End of Mandatory Retirement: Effects on Higher Education.* San Francisco: Jossey-Bass.

Carlson, E.J.
  1990  Mandatory Retirement and the Tenure Contract: A Study of Faculty Retirement Behavior. Paper prepared for the Project on Faculty Retirement. Industrial Relations Section, Princeton University.

Carnegie Foundation for the Advancement of Teaching
  1989  *The Condition of the Professoriate: Attitudes and Trends, 1989.* Princeton, N.J.: Princeton University Press.

Centra, J.A.
  1978  Using student assessments to improve performance and vitality. Pp. 31-49 in W.R. Kirschling, ed., *Evaluating Faculty Performance and Vitality.* New Directions for Institutional Research 20. San Francisco: Jossey-Bass.

Centra, J.A., and F.R. Creech
  1976  *The Relationship Between Student, Teacher, and Course Characteristics and Student Ratings of Teacher Effectiveness.* Report No. PR-76-1. Princeton, N.J.: Educational Testing Service.

Chronister, J.L.
  1990  Characteristics and Costs Related to the Provision of Incentive Early Retirement Plans for Faculty. Paper prepared for the Committee on Manda-

tory Retirement in Higher Education. Center for the Study of Higher Education, University of Virginia.

Chronister, J.L., and B.M. Clevenger

1986a *Early Retirement Programs for Faculty: Three Institutional Case Studies.* Occasional Paper Series #12. Charlottesville, Va.: Center for the Study of Higher Education.

1986b Focus on faculty. *Higher Education and National Affairs* (May 19):5-8.

Chronister, J.L., and T.R. Kepple, Jr.

1987 *Incentive Early Retirement Programs for Faculty: Innovative Responses to a Changing Environment.* Association for the Study of Higher Education-Educational Resources Information Center (ASHE-ERIC) Higher Education Report No. 1. Washington, D.C.: Association for the Study of Higher Education.

Chronister, J.L., and A. Trainer

1985 A case study of the development of an early retirement program for university faculty. *A Journal of Education Finance* 11(2)(Fall):190-204.

Clark, B.R.

1987 *The Academic Life: Small Worlds, Different Worlds.* New York: Carnegie Foundation.

Clark, S.M., M. Corcoran, and D.R. Lewis

1986 The case for an institutional perspective on faculty development. *Journal of Higher Education* 57(2):178.

Commission on Academic Tenure in Higher Education

1973 *Faculty Tenure.* Report and Recommendations of the Commission on Academic Tenure in Higher Education. W.R. Keast and J.W. Macy, Jr., eds. San Francisco: Jossey-Bass.

Commission on College Retirement

1990 *Pension and Retirement Policies in Colleges and Universities: An Analysis and Recommendations.* San Francisco: Jossey-Bass.

Commission on the Future of Community Colleges

1988 *Building Communities: A Vision for a New Century.* Washington, D.C.: American Association of Community and Junior Colleges.

Committee on Assessment of Quality-Related Characteristics of Research-Doctorate Programs in the United States

1982 *An Assessment of Research-Doctorate Programs in the United States.* L.V. Jones, G. Lindzey, and P.E. Coggeshall, eds. Washington, D.C.: National Academy Press.

Consortium on Financing Higher Education (COFHE)

1987 *Early Retirement Programs for Faculty: A Survey of Thirty-Six Institutions.* Cambridge, Mass.: Consortium on Financing Higher Education.

1989 *COFHE Faculty Retirement Benefit Study 1988.* Cambridge, Mass.: Consortium on Financing Higher Education.

Corcoran, M., and S.M. Clark

1989 Faculty Renewal and Change. Pp. 19-32 in G.G. Lozier and M.J. Dooris, eds., *Managing Faculty Resources.* New Directions for Institutional Research 63(Fall). San Francisco: Jossey-Bass.

Covert-McGrath, D.
   1984   NACUBO report: Early and phased retirement. *Business Officer* (June): 13-16.
Daniels, C., and J. Daniels
   1989   College and university pension plans and retirement policies: Current status. *Benefits Quarterly* 5(2):28-39.
   1990a  Retirement and the Professoriate: Questions for Today. Unpublished manuscript. School of Arts and Sciences, Eastern Connecticut State University.
   1990b  Voluntary retirement incentive options in higher education. *Benefits Quarterly* 6(2):68-78.
Douglas, J.M.
   1989   *Directory of Faculty Contracts and Bargaining Agents in Institutions of Higher Education.* New York: National Center for the Study of Collective Bargaining in Higher Education and the Professions, Baruch College, City University of New York.
Eble, K.E., and W.J. McKeachie
   1985   *Improving Undergraduate Education Through Faculty Development: An Analysis of Effective Programs and Practices.* San Francisco: Jossey-Bass.
El-Khawas, E.
   1990   *Campus Trends, 1990.* Washington, D.C.: American Council on Education.
Employee Benefit Research Institute
   1990   *Preservation of Pension Benefits.* Issue Brief 98. Washington, D.C.: Employee Benefits Research Institute.
Faculty Development and Renewal Subcommittee
   1987   The Implications of the Aging of the Faculty in the Health Sciences with Projections of the Distribution of Age with the End of Mandatory Retirement. Report of the Faculty Development and Renewal Subcommittee of the Health Sciences Committee, University of California.
Felicetti, D.A.
   1982   Retirement options to offer college faculty. *Educational Record* (Summer):22-26.
Finkin, M.W.
   1989   Tenure after the ADEA Amendments: A different view. Pp. 97-111 in K.C. Holden and W.L. Hansen, eds., *The End of Mandatory Retirement: Effects on Higher Education.* San Francisco: Jossey-Bass.
Gajda, A.J.
   1989   Long-term care insurance. *Employee Benefits Journal* 14(2):10-16.
Goodman, M.J.
   1990   The review of tenured faculty: A collegial model. *Journal of Higher Education* 61(4):408-424.
Gray, K.
   1989   *Retirement Plans and Expectations of TIAA-CREF Policyholders.* New York: Teachers Insurance and Annuity Association-College Retirement Equities Fund.
Heller, S.
   1986   Colleges ponder the effects on tenure of end to mandatory retirement at 70. *Chronicle of Higher Education* (December 3):15,18.

Holden, K.C., and W.L. Hansen, eds.
   1989  *The End of Mandatory Retirement: Effects on Higher Education* New
         Directions for Higher Education 65 XVII(1). San Francisco: Jossey-Bass.
Holland, D.M.
   1988  Facilitating Faculty Retirement. Unpublished paper. Alfred P. Sloan School
         of Management, Massachusetts Institute of Technology.
Hopkins, D.S.P., and W.F. Massy
   1981  *Planning Models for Colleges and Universities.* Stanford, Calif.: Stanford
         University Press.
Howe, A.B., and S.P. Smith
   1990  Age and Research Activity. Paper prepared for the Project on Faculty
         Retirement, Princeton University.
Hull, D.L., P.D. Tessner, and A.M. Diamond
   1978  Planck's principle. *Science* 202:717-723.
Irish, L., and C. Stewart
   1990  Institutional Responses to the Elimination of Mandatory Retirement. Paper
         prepared for the Committee on Mandatory Retirement in Higher Educa-
         tion. Jones, Day, Reavis, and Pogue, Washington, D.C.
Johnson, B.
   1987  *Public Retirement Systems: Summaries of Public Retirement Plans Cover-
         ing Colleges and Universities—1987.* New York: Teachers Insurance and
         Annuity Association-College Retirement Equities Fund.
Kellams, S.E., and J.L. Chronister
   1988  *Life After Early Retirement: Faculty Activities and Perceptions.* Occa-
         sional Paper No. 1. Center for the Study of Higher Education, Department
         of Educational Leadership and Policy Studies. Charlottesville, Va.: Uni-
         versity of Virginia.
Kinney, D.P., and S.P. Smith
   1989  Age and Teaching Performance. Paper prepared for the Project on Faculty
         Retirement, Princeton University.
Lehman, H.C.
   1953  *Age and Achievement.* Princeton, N.J.: Princeton University Press.
Licata, C.M.
   1985  An Investigation of the Status of Post-Tenure Faculty Evaluation in Se-
         lected Community Colleges. Paper presented at the annual meeting of the
         Association for the Study of Higher Education, Chicago, Ill.
   1986  Post-Tenure Faculty Evaluation: Threat or Opportunity? Association for
         the Study of Higher Education-Education Resouces Information Center Higher
         Education Report No. 1. Washington, D.C.: Association for the Study of
         Higher Education.
Lozier, G.G., and M.J. Dooris
   1988  *Is Higher Education Confronting Faculty Shortages?* Monograph No. 88-
         4. Houston, Tex.: Institute for Higher Education Law and Governance.
   1990  Elimination of Mandatory Retirement: Anticipating Faculty Response. Pa-
         per presented at the convention of the American Society for Higher Educa-
         tion, San Francisco, April 1.

Lozier, G.G., and M.J. Dooris, eds.
1989 *Managing Faculty Resources*. New Directions for Institutional Research 63(Fall). San Francisco: Jossey-Bass.

Mangan, K.S.
1987 Colleges urged to consider tenure contracts with agreed expiration dates. *Chronicle of Higher Education* (April 29):13.

Mauch, J.E.
1990 Looking Forward to Uncapping: A Pilot Inquiry into Costs of Faculty Retirement Benefits and Inducements. Paper prepared for the Committee on Mandatory Retirement in Higher Education. Department of Educational Administration, University of Pittsburgh.

McKeachie, W.J.
1983 Faculty as a renewable resource. Pp. 57-66 in R.G. Baldwin and R.T. Blackburn, eds., *College Faculty: Versatile Human Resources in a Period of Constraint*. New Directions for Institutional Research 40(10):60. San Francisco: Jossey-Bass.

McMorrow, J.A.
1990 Retirement Incentives and Federal Employment Discrimination Law. Paper prepared for the Committee on Mandatory Retirement in Higher Education. Washington and Lee University School of Law.

McPherson, M.S., and G.C. Winston
1988 The economics of academic tenure: A relational perspective. Pp. 174-199 in D.W. Breneman and T.I.K. Youn, eds., *Academic Labor Markets and Careers*. Philadelphia, Pa.: The Falmer Press.

Messeri, P.
1988 Age differences in the reception of new scientific theories: The case of plate tectonics theory. *Social Studies of Science* 18:91-112.

Mooney, C.J.
1988 3 in 4 colleges offer health-care insurance coverage to retired employees, TIAA-CREF survey finds. *Chronicle of Higher Education* (Nov. 30):A17.

Morris, A.A.
1990 A Study of the Legal and Related Aspects of Tenure and Allied Areas in ADEA's Removal of Mandatory Retirement of Tenured Faculty Members Employed by Institutions of Higher Education. Paper prepared for the Committee on Mandatory Retirement in Higher Education. University of Washington School of Law.

Mortimer, K.P., M. Bagshaw, and A.T. Masland
1985 *Flexibility in Academic Staffing: Effective Policies and Practices*. Association for the Study of Higher Education-Education Resources Information Center Higher Education Report No. 1. Washington, D.C.: Association for the Study of Higher Education.

Mulanaphy, J.M.
1984 *Lessons on Retirement: A Statistical Report of the 1982-83 Survey of Retired TIAA-CREF Annuitants*. New York: Teachers Insurance and Annuity Association-College Retirement Equities Fund.

Munnell, A.H., and J.B. Grolnic
1986 Should the U.S. government issue index bonds? *New England Economic Review* (September-October):3-21.

National Center for Education Statistics
  1990a *A Descriptive Report of Faculty in Higher Education.* NCES 90-339. Washington, D.C.: U.S. Department of Education.
  1990b *Faculty in Higher Education Institutions, 1988.* NCES 90-365. Washington, D.C.: U.S. Department of Education.
National Research Council
  1980 *Research Excellence Through the Year 2000: The Importance of Maintaining a Flow of New Faculty into Academic Research.* Commission on Human Resources. Washington, D.C.: National Academy Press.
  1987a Speech understanding and aging. Committee on Hearing, Bioacoustics, and Biomechanics, Commission on Behavioral and Social Sciences and Education. *Journal of the Acoustical Society of America* (3):859-895.
  1987b *Work, Aging, and Vision.* Committee on Vision, Commission on Behavioral and Social Sciences and Education. Washington, D.C.: National Academy Press.
  1989a Methodological Report of the 1987 Survey of Doctorate Recipients. Prepared by M. Belisle, Office of Scientific and Engineering Personnel, National Research Council, Washington, D.C.
  1989b *Surveying the Nation's Scientists and Engineers: A Data System for the 1990s.* C.F. Citro and G. Kalton, eds. Committee on National Statistics, Commission on Behavioral and Social Sciences and Education. Washington, D.C.: National Academy Press.
  1990a *Human Factors Research Needs for an Aging Population* S.J. Czaja and R.M. Guion, eds. Committee on Human Factors, Commission on Behavioral and Social Sciences and Education. Washington, D.C.: National Academy Press.
  1990b Telephone Follow-Up Interviewing to the 1989 Survey of Doctorate Recipients: Results of a Pilot Study. Prepared by S. Mitchell, Office of Scientific and Engineering Personnel, National Research Council, Washington, D.C.
  1991 *Pay for Performance Evaluating Performance Appraisal and Merit Pay.* G.T. Milkovich and A.K. Wigdor, eds. Committee on Performance Appraisal for Merit Pay, Commission on Behavioral and Social Sciences and Education. Washington, D.C.: National Academy Press.
National Science Foundation
  1988 *Proposal Review at NSF: Perceptions of Principal Investigators.* Report of a survey by NSF's program evaluation staff. Washington, D.C.: National Science Foundation.
O'Brien, T., and R. Woodbury
  1988 Retirement Benefits for University Employees: Evaluating the Tradeoffs. Paper prepared as part of a study funded by the Carnegie Corporation of New York. University of Massachusetts at Amherst.
Over, R.
  1989 Age and scholarly impact. *Psychology and Aging* 4(2):222-225.
Patton, C.V.
  1979 *Academia in Transition: Mid-Career Change or Early Retirement.* Cambridge, Mass.: Abt Books.

Powell, D.H.
    1991  Cognitive Aging Among Intellectually Able Individuals:  Overview.  Paper
          presented at the annual meeting of the American Association for the Ad-
          vancement of Science.
Pratt, H.J
    1989  Uncapping mandatory retirement:  The lobbyist's influence.  Pp. 15-31 in
          K.C. Holden and W.L. Hansen, eds., *The End of Mandatory Retirement:
          Effects on Higher Education.*  San Francisco:  Jossey-Bass.
Redway, A.
    1989  Pension indexation—matching challenges and opportunities.  *Employee Benefits
          Digest* 26(10):3-6.
Rees, A., and S.P. Smith
    1991  *Faculty Retirement in the Arts and Sciences.*  Princeton, N.J.: Princeton
          University Press.
Reisman, B.
    1986  Performance evaluation for tenured faculty:  Issues and research *Liberal
          Education,* 72(1):73-87.
Ruth, J.-E., and J.E. Birren
    1985  Creativity in adulthood and old age:  Relations to intelligence, sex and
          mode of testing.  *International Journal of Behavioral Development* 8:99-
          109.
Schaie, K.W., and S.L. Willis
    1986  *Adult Development and Aging.*  2nd ed.  Boston, Mass.:  Little, Brown, and
          Co.
Southworth, J.R., and R.A. Jagmin
    1979  *Potential Financial and Employment Impact of Age 70 Mandatory Retire-
          ment Legislation on COFHE Institutions.*  Cambridge, Mass.: Consortium
          on Financing Higher Education.
Spreadbury, C.
    1984  Innovative plans to encourage senior faculty to take early retirement. *Jour-
          nal of the National Association for Women Deans Administrators and Counselors*
          (Spring):14-20.
Teachers Insurance and Annuity Association-College Retirement Equities Fund (TIAA-
          CREF)
    1989  Target benefit plans.  *Research Dialogues* (22)(July).
    1990  *College and University Employee Benefit and Insurance Benefits Cost Sur-
          vey.*  New York:  Teachers Insurance and Annuity Association College
          Retirement Equities Fund.
University of Minnesota Mandatory Retirement Task Force
    1989  Agenda, November 16 meeting, Mandatory Retirement Task Force.
U.S. Senate
    1978  Senate Report No. 95-493 on the Age Discrimination in Employment Act
          Amendments of 1978.  Pp. 504-536 in United States Code: Congressional
          and Administrative News, 95th Congress—Second Session, Volume 3, Leg-
          islative History.  St. Paul, Minn.:  West Publishing Company.
Watkins, B.T.
    1985  Early-retirement options gaining popularity among colleges and older fac-
          ulty members.  *The Chronicle of Higher Education*  (July 10):19-21.

Weintraub, S., D.H. Powell, D.K. Whitla, R. Catlin, H.H. Funkenstein, and E.F. Kaplan
1991 Patterns of Cognitive Change with Aging in Physicians: Results from Computerized Assessment of Mental State. Paper presented at the annual meeting of the American Association for the Advancement of Science.

White House Conference on Aging
1961 *Policy Statements and Recommendations.* Washington, D.C.: U.S. Department of Health, Education, and Welfare.

Wilner, J.D.
1990 Uncapping Mandatory Retirement in Public, Four-Year Colleges and Universities. Preliminary report. Department of Education, George Washington University.

Zuckerman, H.
1977 *Scientific Elite: Nobel Laureates in the United States.* New York: The Free Press, Macmillan.